RAGING
AGAINST AGING

kicking & screaming, laughing & crying, stretching & kvetching

Jacqueline Becker

ISBN: 1546458344
ISBN 13: 9781546458340
Library of Congress Control Number: 2017907241
CreateSpace Independent Publishing Platform
North Charleston, South Carolina

To my Phil, who has filled my life so that I never feel lonely. To my daughter, who lights up my life. To my grandson, who is the cake. To my granddaughter, who is the icing on the cake.

ACKNOWLEDGMENTS

I owe this book to my editor, my literary angel, Sherry Suib Cohen, who kept me honest and true to myself.

Thank you to Judith Kelman for your unwavering support right from the get-go.

Thank you to my extra pairs of eyes: Terry Austerweil and Rosalie Silver.

A special thank-you to Jasmine Thorson for the final content edit, for eliminating extraneous material.

A heartfelt thank-you to the special person who did my final edit: you know who you are.

TABLE OF CONTENTS

Acknowledgments   v

Orthopedic Shoes And Dinner   1
Upper West Side Vs. Upper East Side   7
Who Will Support Broadway?   16
An Overactive Mind   20
Shoes Again   25
My Mother   33
Jewish Genealogy   36
Why Didn't They Let Her Sing?   39
Conversation On The Couch   42
Amazon Prime   46
The Maintenance Plan   51
My Kitchen   53
"Adult Children" Is An Oxymoron   55
Daily Life: It's All In The Details   58
My Biggest Pet Peeve   63
Forgetting And Remembering   67
Stretching And *Kvetching*   71
A Lot Of Stuff   75
Peach Heaven   82
Boys And Girls   88
Naches   91

Passing The Baton   96
The Garden   98
The New Normal Raises New Questions   104
The Final Chapter   107

ORTHOPEDIC SHOES AND DINNER

We are supposed to feel like we are in our twenties, romantically intertwined, with no obligations. We are supposed to hold hands and walk around the city aimlessly, mindlessly. We are supposed to drink in the energy all around us while losing ourselves looking into each other's eyes.

Oh, we walk around, but we have to make so many pit stops along the way that we change our route to be near the Starbucks and McDonald's. We never make it to Riverside Park. Instead, we stick close to Broadway on the Upper West Side.

It is supposed to be a glorious four days, sunny and warm. But our first day has turned cloudy and windy, with a hint of autumn to come. A voice deep inside wells up, a voice I desperately want to squash.

"You are in the early autumn of your life," it reminds me.

There, it pops out!

We are wandering around and we are not holding hands. Suddenly, we find ourselves standing directly across the street from Harry's, the Upper West Side mecca for people with problematic

1

feet. The store has the facilities my husband desperately needs; plus we both have difficulty finding shoes that fit us comfortably.

I drag my husband in. He immediately goes off to find the bathroom, and I look for shoes. The salesman looks at my feet. I only have two choices. Both pairs of shoes that he is holding up for me to view are made in Germany. These laced-up shoes—one pair standing in for an upbeat walking shoe in black patent leather, the other a brown nubuck that can serve as a boot in the winter—accommodate all eight of my hammertoes *and* my custom orthotics. I wonder just how old my mother was when she started wearing these kinds of shoes. The company touts that these shoes have steel support for both the arches and the metatarsals. They have extra cushioning for the pads of the feet. They are especially designed to help those who suffer from neuropathy from diabetes. I do not suffer from diabetes, but I do have neuropathy, the loss of sensation, in both my legs and feet.

"In Germany," the salesman tells me, "your shoes would be considered medical shoes."

I cannot help it. A voice deep inside me surfaces: I hope these medical shoes are not a result of some of Mengele's "scientific" work. I know this is politically incorrect, and I do not say it out loud. But there is no thought police yet, and if the German Nazis really did not want me to think it, they should never have done what they did.

I inspect the shoes. The truth is that they are cute even though they are actually ugly. They are kind of cool in an offbeat way. They will probably become a conversation piece, a potential ice-breaker. And besides, what choice do I have? They are the only kind that fit me.

I text my husband to find him. While I am trying on my shoes, it seems that my husband has found his own salesman on the other side of the store. My husband is busy trying on supportive sneakers and comfortable, wide dress shoes. The kind you cannot find on the Internet.

I throw in a pair of merino sport socks, and we meet up at the counter. I look at our bill. Together, our bill comes to $1,100.00 and change. Later, I would wish I had bought a dozen of those merino sports socks. They are so comfortable, and once we decided to spend that kind of money, a few more dollars would have been insignificant, really. We ask the store to ship three of the four new pairs of shoes home because we cannot lug them around.

Eleven hundred dollars, I muse. Eleven hundred dollars seems a lot less than one thousand one hundred. "Our hotel—the four nights," I stammer, "is costing us sixteen hundred dollars"

"We need the shoes," my husband reminds me.

"Yes," I agree.

But are old people's shoes romantic? These four days are our twenty-fifth anniversary present to ourselves. Of course, you are supposed to spend on your anniversary. After twenty-five years, you had better spend on your anniversary. But how can romance cost the same as shoes? And can old people's shoes be romantic, let alone sexy? Maybe I should have just gotten some jewelry instead.

I remember that when we first decided to get married, my husband asked me if I wanted a diamond ring or a computer. I thought and thought about it.

"A computer," I answered him. "We'll figure out a way to make more money with the computer, and then we will be able to afford to get a diamond ring for me."

This marriage was not only romantic. I was in my midthirties, and he was in his early forties when we met. This was a second marriage for both of us, and there was more of a sense of economic utilitarianism and practicality this time around. A man I could solve problems with, now, seemed like a romantic choice.

The sky is clearing, and I walk out, wearing my new shoes. They are extremely comfortable. I feel supported. But they are also heavy, and they seem to weigh me down. I never did get that diamond. By the time we could have afforded it, we were working so hard that we both opted for a Caribbean resort vacation instead. Are the memories or the shoes weighing on me?

We go out to eat that evening. We are too tired to keep walking, so we find a place nearby that serves healthy-type food. My husband is not supposed to have any salt; I must watch the carbs. I cannot eat dairy. My husband has to hydrate. My husband also has a cholesterol issue. I tend to watch what *he* eats.

Restaurant food has way more salt than either one of us needs. Because of the extra salt, we drink more water, and because of the extra water, we need to pee even more than usual.

"Are you ready to order?" the waitress asks.

I hold my breath. My husband has a "when we are out, it doesn't count" rule. Clearly he has made that up.

"I will have the sirloin burger," he announces.

I cannot help myself. I begin ticking off "high in cholesterol" in my head.

"French fries or vegetables?" she asks nonchalantly.

I take a deep breath.

"French fries," he answers and quickly adds, "What kind of soup do you have today?"

I begin to pray that he will not find any choice suitable, because soup is loaded with salt, because soup without salt does not taste that good.

"I'll have the chicken soup," he says.

I usually spend two hours a week at the supermarket. I read the salt content of each and every product. One meal out can undo a whole month of my home cooking.

"What?" My husband has read my mind. "It's healthy," he says with a twinkle.

I grew up with women who nagged their husbands to death in order to keep them alive. I never wanted to become one of those women. But I am desperate to keep my husband alive because I desperately do not want to start over. Desperate people do desperate things. I bow my head and silently forgive those women and sigh.

"Would you like to see the dessert menu?" the waitress asks.

"Sure," my husband says without a moment's hesitation.

"*What!*" My husband shrugs looking directly at me. "We're eating out." And he orders the chocolate pecan pie.

"Without the whipped cream," I say. The words have bolted out of my mouth.

The following evening, the weather has warmed up nicely. We both feel lazy. The hotel has a lovely outside dining area, and we plop ourselves down. I throw my shawl over my head. My husband pulls on his sweater. The staff lights the outdoor warmers. There is a constant parade of people going by.

I follow my husband's glance. She might be twenty or thirty. I can no longer tell.

When the waitress comes, I tune out, and instead, I go deep inside my head and remember other ends of summer, other vacations, other restaurant meals. I am too tired to argue about food. Besides, what good will it do me? It will be what it will be, the voice in my head reassures. Don't argue. Just make sure he drinks lots of water.

When the food comes, I will myself not to look at my husband's plate. Instead I look up and around, and by doing so, I have invited what is about to come. It is a game my husband loves to play. He likes to make up stories about the people he sees. He then believes the story he tells and goes on to ask me questions as if what he made up is real. It goes like this:

"See that couple over there?" He points, totally humiliating me. "He's a professor at Columbia. And she is a journalist. How do you think they can afford the city?"

"They live in the same one-bedroom rent-stabilized apartment he moved into when he was in grad school and they chose not to have children," I answer.

"See that guy sitting over there?" My husband points to someone at a nearby table, someone who might or might not be staying at this hotel. "He is here on business. What do you think he does?"

5

I look, and I have no idea. But that is not the way the game we are playing goes. "He is a visiting professor." I sound earnest. "He is here to talk to other intellectuals. He is collecting ideas for his book. It is publish or perish," I continue.

"What is he writing about?"

"Economics," I answer.

"See this couple walking by?" My husband points yet again. She is all but four inches away from me.

"He is a trust-fund baby," I say, and my husband clucks and shakes his head disapprovingly. "He doesn't work," I say to tick him off because my husband cannot fathom such a notion.

"She is studying at Bank Street. He is an art collector. They inherited money, and they live in a fabulous two-bedroom apartment with floor-to-ceiling glass windows that overlook the Hudson on Riverside Drive. They are on a high floor, and they can see straight across the river to New Jersey."

My husband falls silent. Game over.

We go up to our hotel room, and there, right next to the door, is a bottle of champagne on ice—a gift from hotel management. My husband picks up the bottle but does not open it. "Let's save it for tomorrow," he says, putting it in the tiny fridge.

He crawls into bed. "Shower in the morning," he mumbles and falls right to sleep.

UPPER WEST SIDE VS. UPPER EAST SIDE

My husband is snoring next to me. I cannot fall asleep, so I wander off into the sitting room. At night, the mocha-colored walls seem darker—more like espresso. The one window looks smaller especially because of the heavy curtains that drape it on both sides. The lights are too dim. There is no recessed lighting in this hotel room. My feet are naked and exposed. Man, they are really, really ugly. When exactly did this happen? In my twenties, I drew my foot for art class. I framed it, and it is still hanging on our bedroom wall. One commercial that advertises the pill that gives men long-sustaining erections is shot in the desert. Maybe we should have gone to Scottsdale or Taos. We could have gone anywhere. We could have gone to Paris for the long weekend or Boston, Montreal, Chicago, Austin, Toronto. We chose Manhattan.

Of course I bang into the ottoman coffee table! I cannot tell if I have stubbed my toe or toes because the neuropathy does not let me feel pain the way I once did. I cringe and plop myself down on the sofa. I have no idea how this could have happened because the table is an oval. It does not have any straight edges as far as I know. While I am rubbing my foot, I glance toward the window. I get up and stare out and across. Most of the apartments or condos or co-ops—whatever they are—do not have curtains on the windows. A few are still lit. I have just finished reading *Visible City*, by Tova Mirvis, and I want to peep into other people's lives. Unlike the main character in the book, I do not witness anyone having sex. I do not see rooms filled with art and antiques. I do not see bookshelves. I do not see oriental carpets. I do not see anything that can allow me to imagine what my life might have been like had I opted to stay in the city instead of leaving for the suburbs so many years ago. I walk gingerly around the coffee table. I go back to bed, careful not to bump into anything else. At home I learned, like a blind person, to feel my way in the dark, but a hotel room is not home.

The sunlight is pouring in. I go back to sit in the living area with my feet comfortably atop the tufted ottoman—the same ottoman that was my enemy last night. I survey the room. The building is definitely pre–World War I, so the ceilings are high, giving the illusion of space. The sitting room is the size of a standard bedroom. The deep-taupe walls, with the painted enamel black crown moldings, seem so formal. There is a gauche gilded silver mirror with an antique finish hanging near the door. It is not placed exactly opposite the window, so it does not reflect the sunlight. Even with the light pouring in from the window, this room could use more light. There is the perfunctory desk with the office chair. The dark wooden chest has curved drawers, which are decorated with painted flowers. The drapes are striped—gold and white with a matching valance sporting inverted pleats. Golden tassels hang across the valance like the paper chains we used to make in grade school. Heavy-duty golden tassels hold the heavy drapes open.

Mais oui, the hotel, *certainement*, is French. The room must have been recently remodeled. I can see that the carpet has no stains.

The tufted oval ottoman is meant to look like leather but smells of vinyl. I finally find the culprit—this ottoman coffee table has curlicue wrought iron feet that stick out beyond the top. They blend in with the carpet, and in the dim light, they cannot be seen. I make a mental note to try to remember those damn curlicue feet. But then I begin to worry that by evening, I will have forgotten this warning, because I seem to be forgetting things a lot now.

My husband offers to run out and bring back breakfast. A croissant will certainly go perfectly with the French theme, but I am lactose intolerant. So my husband sweetly offers to walk the block and a half to the gourmet shop to ensure that I can have soy milk and a roll that is not made with dairy products.

He leaves, and I am struck by a memory of a vacation twenty-five years earlier. We had gotten back to the hotel in the late evening then, too. He closed the door behind us. He scooped me up from behind. He began kissing my earlobes, fondling me. He drew me down to the floor, gently but firmly. He commanded my attention. And he took me tenderly, as he took my breath away. The very next morning, he went out and came back with breakfast just as I was setting the table with coffee.

He was handsome and charismatic. He was confident and fun. And our life together lay entirely ahead of us. I was in love. I was so hopeful. Everything felt easy. I thought we could solve every problem.

Divorce had wreaked havoc on both of us. I came out of my divorce feeling like a World War II survivor. My husband came out of his divorce feeling like a Sioux after Sitting Bull had been defeated and the hunt was over. Climbing back took so much longer than I ever imagined. There is a saying that a recession is a depression when it happens to you. My husband was caught up in a series of mergers and acquisitions in a time that the advertising industry was collapsing. He opened his own studio, but he was trying to succeed in advertising during the recession that hit after Black Monday

1987. All his good work ethic, enthusiasm, high hopes, and experience did not get him back in the saddle. People-in-the-know know that the creative fields are the first to go in economic downturns. We were two creative people starting over later in life, and there were no jobs. I had no idea then how hard it would be, the compromises we would have to make, the amount of time it would take to recoup what we lost in the aftermath of our individual divorces.

As I look around at the room, the walls seem to be caving in. The decor is reminiscent of another time and place. Perhaps it was ludicrous to come to Manhattan only to be tricked into pretending that I was in Versailles in its heyday, when France was at its height of opulence and beauty, when Europe ruled, when I was in my prime. I was thirty-five years old when we met. I was thirty-eight when we married. Only twenty-five short years and a lifetime ago.

My husband comes back. We eat. It is time to get out and walk around. We walk to the bus stop. I don't mention that seniors can ride for half price. We came to the city to escape the obvious, and my husband certainly does not want me to remind him that we are aging. "Does it make you feel better to talk about it?" he chastised me the last time I tried to broach the subject. "Work will help us stay young" is still his mantra.

Only I don't want to work so hard anymore. The problem is that all my husband has to give substance to his life is his work, and I myself am having trouble finding a real substitute for the work from which I have since retired.

Everyone on the bus appears to be wearing muted, muddy colors, grays, beiges, and institutional greens. Their faces have that NYC don't-look-at-me look. They all look like workers. The word "proletariat" pops up from an English lit class I took years and years ago.

My husband must be reading my mind, because he leans over and whispers in my ear, "How are they making it in New York City? Where do they live?" And he continues, "How can they afford the rent? What do they do for a living?"

I let him ask and answer his own questions because the truth is, he is whispering in my ear, and his hot breath feels so nice and tingly.

"They all look like they wear uniforms for a living," he concludes.

"Yes," I reply. "This is a crosstown bus, and we are going east. They probably work in the hospitals or at the doctors' offices."

Even though we are celebrating our anniversary, we are combining business with pleasure, and we are, indeed, on the way to one of my husband's doctors to check on his growing prostate gland. We are seeking a second opinion, because I, secretly or not so secretly, want to make sure—100 percent—that he does not have prostate cancer.

I watch a boy board the bus with his mother. Somehow they stand apart from the others on the bus. For starters, they are extremely well dressed. She is wearing a classic pinstripe skirt and smart high-heeled pumps. The shoes look brand new, but you can tell she feels comfortable in them. Her hair is pulled back and up, and she exudes confidence. Her son is wearing a helmet, and he is carrying a scooter. He observes everything, and as we travel under the overpass, he remarks that the arches are made from stone. His dark-brown, alert eyes miss nothing. Both mother and son scream Upper West Side sophistication. It is obvious that even though this boy may only be four years old, he is already part of the city. He belongs. We get off at the last stop.

We are in the medical center of New York City. The doctors here can perform miracles. They are specialists who specialize in specifics. It hardly seems fair. My husband suffered from severe spinal stenosis in his lower back for years. We used to walk from one Starbucks to another to another so that my husband could sit down and rest. Then it got so bad he could not walk even one-quarter of a city block without sitting down. He had surgery on this very block, in this very hospital, just last year. He walked out of Weill Cornell the next morning and has been walking ever since. Only now his *new* condition is so bad that we cannot walk a block before he has to pee. And so we are back to walking from Starbucks to Starbucks to Starbucks again, simply to use their restrooms.

It turns out that my husband's growing condition is normal and is a natural part of the process he does not want to name. Who knew that the only gland that keeps growing in old age is the prostate gland? The specialist in the city who deals with this normal yet terribly annoying condition prescribes yet one more pill that should help this problem.

We play the game What If. What if we win the lottery? Of course we cannot, because my husband does not believe in "gambling," so he does not buy lottery tickets. I sneak and buy them whenever I come into the city alone.

"The first thing I would do," my husband says, "is buy an apartment in the city."

I know he would buy it on the Upper West Side. The Upper West Side has a reputation of being more down to earth than the Upper East Side, more professional, more creative, more intellectual, more liberal.

In a heartbeat, I would look for an apartment on the Upper East Side. It is newer. It is the medical hub, and as I am aging, I know to count the seconds it would take to get in and out of an ambulance to the best hospital in the tri-state area. It is true that there are museums all over New York City. But the Upper East Side has the biggest, the best, and the most.

My husband lived on the Upper West Side when he first moved to New York from the Midwest. He lived there when he married his first wife, and he only left for the suburbs after they had their second child. One of my best friends moved to the Upper East Side. I love the shopping. If I win the lottery, I will indeed be rich, but in the meantime, I prefer not to have to pretend anything at my age.

Now that we can celebrate legitimately, we head over to the Frick Museum. I am a native-born New Yorker and have never been here, even though I studied art so many years ago. The Frick is magnificent, breathtaking.

My husband is animated and whispering rather loudly, "This Frick! He was a robber baron along with Andrew Carnegie."

He is so excited that he can relate this expedition to history. I stop and stare at the Rembrandt. I have seen this portrait many times in art books but never in real life. *The Matadors*, by Manet, is a fascinating composition. I know in a split second that the Whistlers on the wall were influenced by Japanese paintings. Now it is my husband's turn to be impressed by my knowledge of art history.

For a minute I cannot or do not want to recall why I gave up painting so long ago. I can feel the brushstrokes, the colors, the way Turner's yellows and blues create sunlight on the canvas. The three Vermeers alone are worth the trip. The delicate figures that emerge out of the dark are exquisite. After studying the portraits by Holbein and Goya and their strong compositions, my eyes are drawn to the carpets and the furniture. Such attention to detail. Such craftsmanship. Such pride in workmanship. Why on earth did humanity ever invent machines? Will robots take away more and more jobs? Without work, can there be purpose? And without purpose, can life be worth living? Is that what my husband means by "work will keep me young?" Without a sense of pride and purpose, would he wither away? And why can't I find something meaningful to take the place of the career from which I retired? I was not ready to stop working, and yet, I could no longer get up at five o'clock in the morning. I could no longer handle driving the long distance in the bad weather. I did not want to keep up with the new technology. I could no longer teach social-emotional literacy like it was an academic subject. Is this what limbo feels like?

We take selfies under the pillars in the interior courtyard. I dub them "Frick and Frack at the Frick." But later we post them on our tutoring website. We post that we are sitting under the pillars of Knowledge and Wisdom. My husband may represent Knowledge in our family unit. He certainly knows his history inside out. But clearly, I represent Wisdom, knowledge that has come to me through the School of Hard Knocks and Experiences.

"Can we take this trip as a write-off?" I ask my husband. "I mean, we just created our next ad."

In my book, wisdom is defined as practical knowledge.

We walk to the crosstown bus. We wait in line. We board the crowded bus. Two young girls offer their seats. I look behind me to see whom they are talking to. My husband is standing right behind me. The young women are in the process of getting up. Their seats are empty. I am confused. In a split second, the opportunist in me goes for the seats. Somehow, I manage to whisper a thank-you, but for the duration of the ride back to the hotel, I am preoccupied. Was it my gray roots? Was it my wrinkled face? Was it my orthopedic shoes? I look down at my feet. The shoes *are* cute in an ugly way, I reassure myself.

My mind wanders, and I remember my girlfriend's son's wedding. It was just last year, a black-tie affair for the family members, dressy for the guests. It was not difficult for me to find a lavender ruched cocktail dress that made my figure look good and brought out my lavender-blue eyes. Then I looked down at my feet. I did not know what to do. I had worn low-heeled cork sandals to my own daughter's wedding, and that was several years earlier. I went online and ordered a pair of cork-bottom flat silver sandals that I knew were too sporty for the event, but what choice did I have? My husband put on his black sneakers. We arrived early and sat down in the lobby with a glass of wine. From my vantage point, I had the opportunity to look at everyone's feet as they entered the lobby. I spotted one woman hiding a pair of silver loafers under a royal blue gown. Another woman sported a pair of sneakers under her red-sequined pants outfit. Why isn't anyone making silver flat comfortable Mary Janes in a stretchy fabric with a glitzy button? Don't think I did not beg for something like that when I was at Harry's! Naot? Finn? Aetrex? Is *anyone* listening?

We get off the bus and go up to the hotel suite. This time I tiptoe around the coffee table/ottoman. My husband goes into the bedroom and closes his eyes. No matter where we are or what time of day it is, my husband falls asleep just like that.

It is time for another dinner. I gently wake my husband from his nap. No matter how tired, no matter how long or short a nap he takes, no matter how well or how poorly he has slept, my husband always wakes up fully, and he is always in a happy mood. He is so sweet natured that I am tempted to bend over and kiss him. He probably would mistake this tender gesture, and we might never get to dinner. I remember that once upon a time, not so long ago, that had flattered and excited me. Two years before, after my friend Shelley was diagnosed with terminal brain cancer, she said to me in confidence, "Now that the lovemaking is over, I just want to be loved."

I had no idea what she was talking about then. Now I am at a point where I just want to eat and sleep. I am tired of taking care of others. I, too, just want to be taken care of.

WHO WILL SUPPORT
BROADWAY?

The next (and the last) day of our anniversary staycation, we get ready for the finale. Bryant Park is full of people. A lot of working people from the surrounding office buildings come to play Ping-Pong, chess, and other board games. There are kiosks of fast food. There are public restrooms with long lines. There are jugglers and a carousel. It is one of my favorite places to relax and feel energized simultaneously. You cannot help but feel young when you sit among the lunch crowd.

Not long after we met, twenty-seven years ago, my husband, then boyfriend, handed me two tickets, one for my daughter and one for me, to join him on a trip to Ohio to meet his family of origin. He insisted on driving me all over Dayton, Ohio. He pointed to ball field after ball field after ball field.

"I played here when I was nine years old. I played here when I was in seventh grade. I played here the summer before I went to high school. I played here my freshman year of high school. I played here when I was a junior," he told me. He was obviously proud of himself.

When we got back home, I booked an all-day walking tour around New York City.

"I worked here and here and here and here and here..." I said as I pointed to every building where I had once held a job, even a part-time job, because work is work. It became a standard joke between us. He was social chairman of his frat house and claimed that was a job. I have been really working since I started babysitting when I was eleven years old. As we are leaving Bryant Park, I point to yet another building where I once held a summer job.

Now, we are finally on our way to see Idina Menzel! Broadway is the real reason we chose the French hotel for our stay. It is a short walk from the Upper West Side to Broadway, and we both love Broadway.

The seats we purchased at TKTS are really decent. Idina belts out how her life would have turned out *If/Then*. She sings about two different scenarios. Idina herself is forty-one and newly divorced with a son. For all I know, she may just be belting out her own *If/Then* on stage. I remembered *If/Then* was on my mind a lot when I was forty; at fifty, not so much, because by the time I turned fifty, the past did not matter to me. I was so involved in life, I simply did not have any extra time to spare thinking about what-if. Just as the show suggests, I got over it, shrugged my shoulders, accepted that my life was never meant to be perfect, and forgave myself.

The best song in the show, "What the Fuck," sums it up. You never really understand why you messed up, but you learn to just go with it and laugh at your own flawed humanity. At sixty, if I could sing, I would be singing "What the Fuck *Now*," because after sixty, you live waiting for the other shoe to drop.

During intermission, I run to try to be at the head of the line— *the* line to the women's bathroom. It is a common joke about the women's bathroom during intermission. There are hundreds of women waiting to get into the very limited stalls. I look at everyone in front of me. I turn and look behind me. I see a sea of heads. The women are all middle-aged. Their hair is dyed or gray or a combination of gray roots showing at the base of dyed hair. The faces are wrinkled. Some have stopped trying to cover up. Others have on way too much makeup. The baby boomers are supporting the matinees, I realize. All our children are at work. Has this always been the case? What will happen to Broadway when we are no longer able to attend? The questions keep popping into my brain because at sixty-plus, I have become obsessed with passing culture on and down through the generations.

It is a relief to find out that either way, Idina's character's life would have turned out okay. We exit and pass the stage door. There are buses waiting—for whom? For people from assisted-living facilities? Yes, probably. It was not long ago that my mother was in assisted living. I remember she took trips on occasion. But the young people are all standing around behind the barriers. I am no dope. I go where the young people are.

The actors and actresses come out one at a time. They walk down the line and let the ones in line take selfies with them. They autograph the playbills. I am at one with these groupies, even if I feel like a vampire feeding off the flesh of vibrant beings. I, too, wait in line, hold out my playbill, flash a picture. Idina Menzel comes out. She begins to walk down the line. I take her photograph and get her autograph. I have always had backup plans and backup to my backup plans. Should Social Security benefits get cut, I can always sell these on eBay, I tell myself.

But really all I want to do, but dare not, is to cup her cute youngish face and say, "Idinala"—because she is one of us, a nice Jewish girl from Queens and Syosset—"please tell me you have a plan in place for your retirement, because when you are sixty, it must be very hard to belt out your soul on stage once a day, five days a week for evening performances, and an additional twice-a-day, two times a week for matinee performances."

We board our train, and as soon as we sit down, I turn to my husband, and just like that, our anniversary jaunt comes to an end.

"Phil, you have to call Abe again. You have to press upon him that he will be middle-aged in three years. He isn't Idina Menzel. He cannot be sixty and running from gig to gig with no Social Security, no pension, and no money to fix broken teeth. He is thirty-seven and still living with his mother, and he does not have a day job."

My husband knows this. He is frustrated with his youngest child, the son who lost out the most because of his divorce. I suggest that he fly Abe up from Alabama over Abe's next lull, in between his gigs, so that we can hash it out with him face-to-face.

AN OVERACTIVE MIND

Two years ago, we took the doctors at their word. They told us: "It would not be a big deal." I was still working and had only one day left to take off. So we tried to combine business with pleasure then, too. There was nothing wrong with our intent, but the execution was disastrous.

We scheduled my husband's radioactive iodine treatment for thyroid cancer for the morning so that we could still have a nearly full day left for pleasure. My husband told me he had planned a surprise. So when the business part was done, we hopped a cab, and Phil asked the driver to take us to the MOMA. My husband wanted us to celebrate my birthday. He was glad his operation had been a success. He was delighted that the acute gout he had developed as a complication from the surgery was now behind him. He was happy that now that he had taken the radioactive iodine pill, he would not need any other follow-up therapy. He knew that I loved the café at the museum. He recognized that I loved the views from the windows. He knew that I loved the food they serve. He knew how I loved feeling rich.

What neither of us knew then was that the effect of the radioactive iodine was immediate. Phil took one bite of the gourmet dish we had ordered, and he could not swallow. We ran home, and I called for a home-care aide. He suffered for the next ten days. He felt his whole throat was on fire. He had to sleep in isolation for several days. His radioactively contaminated bedding, clothing, even his hairbrush had to be either washed separately or thrown out. I opted to throw them out. We did not yet know that the first operation would only be a partial success; he would need another one the following year. It took almost a whole month for him to feel better.

So the following month, for my husband's birthday, we went to see Neil Sedaka perform at the Westbury Music Fair. Neil Sedaka looked pretty agile, for a man his age, as he shuffled on stage for a full seven minutes before he was too winded to go on. He sang "Calendar Girl," and we went wild. He sang "Oh, Carol," and we went wild. Then he sang "I Miss the Hungry Years," and we sighed.

After intermission, he started to sing his new songs from his new album. They were extremely poignant songs about aging. We couldn't exit the place fast enough. As we dashed out, I looked over my shoulder. I did not see anyone standing in line to purchase his new CD.

But I, too, have become obsessed with aging. It is all I think about. It was only a split-second ago that I worked two jobs (three, if you count the summer), had my house gutted and redone, ripped out every blade of grass, and planted a perennial garden to replace the front lawn. I am in a state of shock. I do not understand how and when this happened to me. I cannot engage anyone to talk about it. So I am writing about it.

My husband may be suffering from an overactive bladder. But clearly, I am suffering from an overactive mind. My mind flits back and forth between present and past. Maybe 9/11 was the wake-up call, or maybe it was the combination of aging plus 9/11, but my husband became obsessed with passing culture down, too. He began teaching in a Sunday school program for post–bar mitzvah boys. He knew what an uphill battle that group would be, so he devised a history lesson and called it "From Moses to Mel Brooks." He taught Judaism and Jewish history through the movies.

After that, he began tutoring. He has become obsessed with teaching American history, grammar, and essay writing. He is determined to get his students into the best colleges. He studies the guidebooks. He counsels the parents, most of whom are foreign born. His dream and their American dream meld. It was both our separate dreams when we were in our twenties. He wanted to go to Columbia. I wanted to go to Barnard. Neither his parents nor mine were willing to take out loans to make that happen. My husband and I share a lot in common.

I joined my husband in the tutoring business just before I retired. I work hard at getting the younger students to read the classics, not the fluff. I am determined to teach literary analysis even to preschoolers, because I still believe that brains are too precious to waste. Out of all the headlines and films out there, it was the movie *Idiocracy* that sounded the alarm for me. At best it is a B movie. The plot is fairly lame. The actors are okay. The premise is that the guy with average intelligence, who was frozen, wakes up in the future and is revered as a genius. He is the only one who knows how to save the rest of humanity, because they are hooked on video games and eat junk food and have lost their ability to think. The people in power have forgotten a basic key concept upon which their survival depends. I find myself recommending that movie to anyone and everyone.

When my daughter became a mother, she became obsessed with children's books. We searched for her favorites. We found some in storage in the attic. We bought some online, used, because they are out of print. We were willing to pay as much as seventy-five dollars a copy. We bought Jewish holiday books. We bought the whole Shalom Sesame series. We bought *Prince of Egypt*. We continue to buy. My daughter and son-in-law named my grandson Graham after their combined favorite author Graham Greene. There are expectations implied.

There are over five thousand years of culture to pass down. There is no time to waste. I may be past my prime, but Amazon is clearly in its prime. Every day another prime package arrives. I can find nearly anything I need to enrich my grandson and granddaughter. And when I cannot, I search the Internet. I found a brontosaurus Chanukah menorah for my grandson. He was three at the time, and of course, he was wholly absorbed in dinosaurs. I found *T. rex* Shabbat candlesticks to light with him when he sleeps over on weekends. I purchased the Sydney Taylor's *All-of-a-Kind Family* series to read with my granddaughter when she will be eight. She is only one, but those books were out of print for so long, I did not want to chance not finding them again. I am already planning our trip to the Tenement Museum on the Lower East Side, as I pray that I will still be able to walk up those stairs by the time she will be ready. My husband attends the synagogue on High Holy Days and actually sits because my grandson sits next to him. My grandson goes up to the *bimah*, the altar, with his grandpa to open the Ark. We are buying my husband his first *tallis*, or prayer shawl. And we sing "Shabbat Shalom" on Friday nights.

We tutor, and we hand money over to my daughter to send our grandson to art lessons and swimming lessons. We tutor, and we hand money over to my daughter to get our granddaughter music lessons because, unlike everyone on our side of the family, this little girl has rhythm and loves to sing and dance.

We arrive home. Four days of mail are piled on our dining-room table. My husband runs out for some groceries. The second I find myself alone in my house (honestly, have you ever heard a woman call it *"our* house?"), I open my closet door. I am very proud of my closet. It stands where an old run-down shed that serviced the garden tools existed when we first bought the cottage. The door opened to the outside. The tiny beach cottage, which was built in 1924, had makeshift shallow closets that were added as it was converted to year-round living quarters. I figured out a way to keep the costs down. I simply lived with a mess.

One day, however, I looked at the shed and looked at the adjacent bedroom wall and a plan emerged. I put money away, a little at a time, and I drew a floor plan. I submitted it myself to the village hall. I used the exact footing of the shed so our taxes would not increase. We had a three-foot footing dug out and concrete block put in. We accessed the closet from the inside. The cathedral ceiling added extra storage capacity. It became a four-foot-deep by eight-foot-wide by nine-and-a-half-foot-high, to the tip, cedar closet. I drove out to Home Depot and got a closet system, and our contractor-neighbor installed it. I have cubbies for shoes and shelves. I even bought the velvet-covered skinny hangers to maximize the space. I threw an oriental carpet that I won on eBay on the floor.

The bedroom is small, but the closet has enough space for all my clothes.

I like feeling rich.

SHOES AGAIN

I open the shoeboxes from Harry's. I got rid of all my low-heeled shoes years ago when the doctor first told me that my arches had fallen. Then my big toes started tingling, and I cringed whenever a summer sheet covered them. Then my feet went completely numb—from my toes up to my ankles. I simply could not feel them. Acupuncture restored minor feeling, but, like a fakir, I can walk on fire without flinching. How do I know? Because several years ago, I stepped on a piece of glass and never felt it. I only found out when I saw the trail of blood on my newly washed kitchen floor.

So I replaced all my cute and somewhat sexy shoes with more utilitarian cork-bottom shoes and sandals that supported my arches. I still have some of them in my closet, and they are simply taking up space because I can no longer wear even those.

But I am a woman, and therefore, I am defined by my footwear. How do I know? Because once, when I started a new job, a whole year and three months passed before a colleague spoke to me, and the first words she ever said to me were "Oh, what cute shoes!" I still remember which ones they were. They were olive-green leather loafers with tassels and sported a designer name. I purchased them at the outlet mall in Lee, Massachusetts. They perfectly matched my olive-green corduroy skirt that I was wearing with my olive-green tights. I looked preppy, and that look won her approval. And because she was a popular teacher, I was now recognized, if not accepted.

I find myself remembering my first pair of low-heeled shoes. I was in eighth grade, and it was almost graduation. We had to wear white. The dress had a tight waist and a flared skirt because that was the style back then. The long-sleeved dress was lace over white satin with a scooped neck. I was very pleased with it. I had short bangs and long hair that ended in a flip. I was trying to look like Jacqueline Kennedy before she became an Onassis. My mother had bought me white silk generic low heels—the kind you buy when you need to have a pair of shoes to match the bridal-party color. I was self-conscious; the boys were all still short, and I was long and lanky, and I teeter-tottered over their heads as I made my way to the prom. Maybe if I had an older, bigger sister at my side, I would have felt less gawky.

Had I known then that I would *really* age, because the inevitable did not seem to apply until I turned sixty, I might have saved all my favorite shoes. Had I done that, I might have put my house up for sale and bought a loft in a gritty area, a place where artists might eventually move to. The walls and high ceilings would be painted a light industrial gray; the pipes would be left exposed, and I would, artfully, display my shoes. "WALK IN *MY* SHOES," I would call this exhibit. My show would be a retrospective of Everywoman. I would never even have to date the shoes. Every woman would know just by looking at them. The exhibit would depict the story of my life. The shoes would take up the positive space. The negative space would be filled by one's imagination. It is an ingenious idea, I decide, because I dare not share this notion of my exhibit with anyone but myself.

Certainly my graduation heels would have been included. They would have been followed by a pair of low black stacked heeled shoes that had two buttons. Now that I am thinking about them, they might have passed for shoes the Pilgrims had worn, but when I was sixteen, I was allowed to wear those stacked heeled shoes to school. They were cute, and I bought them in the Shoe Box, *the* upscale store, on the then-swanky Kings Highway, in Brooklyn. Now you can find the Shoe Box on the Upper East Side. They were expensive. And Harold Mackenstein had gone crazy over them!

I was a junior in high school, but I was dating a freshman in college. He was dark and had a prominent nose. He was not good looking, but he was charismatic and bright and funny, and I was in love. I did not tower over him in this pair of heels, even though he was sort of short, and he adored them. When he called to ask me out (as if I would ever say no), he asked me to wear my black-and-white tweed empire-waisted dress with the black velvet collar and *those* shoes. I preferred black tights with the outfit, but Harold specifically requested that I wear my white tights. He was already that kind of man at twenty. And so I did, when we went to Junior's on Flatbush Avenue to have a slice of cheesecake or ice cream. Harold did not have access to a car. So he would pick me up, and we would go by train or bus or walk to a movie or a show or a dance or whatever he had planned for that Saturday night. He never asked me what I wanted to do. He would prepare me by calling me every Tuesday night to let me know what to expect. He was president of his fraternity. He was a man with a plan. He was easy to talk to and laugh with. He got my jokes. And then after ten months, he wanted to get beyond first base. It turned out that I would not be ready for sex for another two years. And the relationship came to an end. It would be another eighteen years before I met another man who had a similar dark complexion and easygoing and engaging temperament.

Next in line, I would display my brown leather Israeli sandals that I loved because they were so in style the summer that I had climbed Masada in the desert. The leather straps eventually broke, and the soles wore out by the time I had to discard them.

Unfortunately, I would have to add my dumpy white nurse's shoes with laces. I put myself through Brooklyn College working for my own dentist, Dr. Beckenstein. I loved the job because I did it all, from answering the phones to developing the x-rays in the darkroom. Then Dr. Beckenstein tried to persuade me to go to tech school to become a dental hygienist, and soon after I rejected that notion, he tried hard to set me up with his son. It was time to find another job, I remember thinking.

Next in the procession, my red suede low-heeled pumps would tell the story of my early twenties, when I pounded the pavement in Manhattan. I wore them with my pinstripe gray suit. I felt so powerful being a part-time assistant to a one-man employment agency on Park Avenue South. (Why on earth did my boss tell me that he had an affair with a "very nice" Spanish-speaking woman, whom he later placed as a maid? Why do I know that he bought her a mink coat as a thank-you? And why is this something that I will always remember but never fully understand, yet I will take it to my grave?)

In the lineup, there would be my sneakers that served as my pregnancy shoes. I gained thirty-eight pounds and never lost them. Maybe that is why my arches eventually collapsed.

But then, following those dirty plain white sneakers, a pair of high-top sneakers would stand out. They were checkered—orange and khaki and white and olive green. They served as my debut back into the dating world after my divorce. My second husband-to-be, who did not know it yet, had been intrigued by those high-tops. He had totally misunderstood their purpose. They were only a fashion statement, an announcement of sorts that I was back in the game. He had mistaken me for an athlete, not an artsy woman trying to look cool. We met for the first time at an annual event that the 92nd Street Y sponsored—a picnic and softball game in Central Park for newly and not-so-newly divorced parents. It was called Kindred Spirits, a name that made me want to gag.

I had already joined Parents without Partners in the burbs. But when I handed over my application and required fee, I saw that the men who were interviewing me were missing some teeth. (Why were they all men who were interviewing me? Were they screening? Was each one hoping to get the best for himself? Did each one smile, secretly thinking, If I get this one, I can get my teeth fixed?) As I was paying my dues, and I clearly was paying my dues, I knew I was never going to participate in what I now dubbed the "Parents without Teeth" organization. I had already gone to a few Friday nights for single parents at C. W. Post. Before each performance, the host would take pity on us—the newly divorced, the lonely, the deserted, the abandoned, the losers, the ones who had failed. After a few times, I fought back, and I stopped going. After all, *I* was the one who threw my first marriage out.

Before that, I had grabbed another recently divorced friend, and we went out to the hospital in Syosset. We joined a weekly therapy session for the newly separated. It was supposed to be an adult version of Banana Splits, the program social workers run in elementary schools for the children of newly divorced parents. We arrived ten minutes late and walked in while the first person was telling his story. Evidently, he found out he had a terrible disease right after his wife filed for divorce. The second person went on to explain how he ended up with a heart attack. The third person, a woman, developed an autoimmune disease. I kicked my friend under the table and whispered, "If I wanted to find someone sick, I would just go upstairs to one of the wards." And I tugged at her. "Run, run for your life," I said. And we did.

I was so depressed I asked my mother for help. I was so depressed, she actually agreed. "If I am going to meet someone," I explained, "then I might as well meet someone who can afford a vacation." My mother gave me the money for that vacation, and I took my daughter to Club Med over Passover/Easter, or the politically correct spring break. Unfortunately, it was Family Week—that is, couples with children. Fortunately, there was one other single parent there with her son. We hung out together. She told me about Kindred Spirits. The married women took me under their wings. They were empathic and validated that I was not the type to be divorced. They, too, encouraged me to try Kindred Spirits. Who makes up these names? I mean, "MEET Market" might be a bit crass, but at least it would not imply pity. But my mind digresses...

I remember it was a Sunday late in May. I drove into the city and found parking right on Fifth Avenue. To me, my checkered high-tops screamed:

I am not looking for a one-night stand or an affair. I am fun and still hot, and I am only thirty-five. Come and get me! I am looking for a real relationship—willing to work hard and play hard. I want what I just lost—a life in the suburbs as a working mom, but within the context of a *working* relationship. I only need one man.

When I got divorced, it was before the Internet dating sites existed, and my sneakers were my own personal ad.

The first man I bumped into at the annual Kindred Spirits picnic for the divorced and lonely single parents started a one-sided conversation about the weather. Dear God, the voice deep inside me screamed. If I had wanted to talk about the weather, I would have called my mother, a woman who had had a crush on Tex Antoine, and had brushed her hair one hundred strokes a night, totally fixated on the meteorologist, who was later fired after he appeared on television too drunk to forecast the weather, thus leaving her devastated.

A tall man with a darkish complexion, curly black hair, bushy eyebrows, and twinkly warm brown eyes appeared from nowhere.

He was carrying the book *What They DON'T Teach You at Harvard Business School*. He asked me what position I wanted to play in the softball game. I looked at him like he had ten heads, and then I pointed to the book, and somewhere from deep inside, just like that, I started ranting:

"I bet they don't teach you at Harvard Business School that you are going to end up almost middle aged and divorced. I bet they don't teach you at Harvard Business School that you are going to end up alone and have to put a roof over your kid's head. I bet they don't teach you at Harvard Business School that after twelve years of trying to make your marriage work, your marriage would end in the therapist's office, when you looked at your then-husband and asked, 'Do you want me? Do you want the marriage?' and he answered, 'I don't know what I want for breakfast.' 'Then forget dessert' just popped out of your mouth, and right then and there you ended your marriage. Just like that!"

And suddenly, just like that, I stopped talking. I was out of breath.

"I loved being married," this man said, and quickly added, "not to my ex-wife. I mean, I loved the idea of going to sleep with the same woman and waking up next to her every morning."

"What's your name?" I couldn't help but ask.

"Phil," he answered.

What I did know then was that Phil was going to fill my life for better or for worse.

One more pair of shoes would simply have to be included. That would have to be a pair of pale-pink floral cloth sandals with a low wedge heel that I had found at a cheap outlet store in Miami Beach on the first vacation we took as a blended family. My purchase was easy and worked out well. I felt like a movie star from the fifties the minute I put them on. I wore those shoes until the fabric tore apart. The blended-family part—well, even after twenty-five years, we are still working on it.

I would have to add my Naot leather shoe-boots—two pairs: one brown, one black. They are the last vestiges of normalcy that still remain in my closet. Neither pair has laces. They are cut like boots and stitched like boots, but they only go up to the ankle. The brown pair has buckles that close right under the ankle. The black pair has a zipper on the side near the ankle and a thick sole and heel. In fact, upon further inspection, they remind me of my black stacked heeled shoes that I wore for Harold Mackenstein when I was sixteen. They are not sexy, but they are funky, and I still love them. I wore them under pants, of course. But I also dared to wear them with tights and straight skirts. With the right sweater and jewelry, I fancied that I had looked like an interesting character, someone who could not easily be ignored—a cross between Annie Hall and Doris, of Sally Field's unforgettable *Hello, My Name Is Doris*. I simply can never part with either pair because perhaps one day, I *will* get all eight hammertoes operated on. Until then, I will have to wear these German medical shoes.

MY MOTHER

I am an only child. I always wished I had a sister. I could have pretended her name was Johanna. I have always loved that name. Johanna and I would get together for a cup of coffee twice a month—just the two of us. We would share DNA stories and laugh. I got Mom's fucked-up feet. You got Mom's premature white hair. I got Dad's space between the teeth. You got Mom's arthritis. I got Dad's bad eyesight. Hopefully neither of us will get Mom's cancer. We could laugh and cry, remembering.

At sixty-five, my mother went in for a routine hysterectomy and called me from the hospital to tell me that she "had a touch of cancer." She assumed it was uterine cancer. It had turned out to be mesenchymal sarcoma in a fibroid at the back of her uterine wall. It is a very rare and unusually aggressive kind of cancer, and Sloan Kettering put her at a 25 percent chance of making it. They would not treat her.

She did survive. She survived the surgery and the chemo, and she went on to live another twenty-six years. She survived breast cancer at the age of seventy-two. She survived a rare form of noncontagious TB at eighty-two. She had to take megadoses of two very potent antibiotics for eighteen months. As a result, she developed a yeast infection and lost twenty-five pounds. She managed to cure that yeast infection by eating Activia yogurt. A few years later, she fell and broke her back. While she was recuperating, she developed shingles. Then, and only then, did she retire from her part-time job. She was eighty-seven years old at the time.

She sent herself to an assisted-living facility. She had been suffering from Parkinson's disease the whole time. In the facility, she caught her toe in her pajama pant, fell, and broke her hip. She went to a rehab center and came out stronger than when she had gone in. She called me one day with news.

"I met a younger man."

My silence disturbed my mother.

"Don't you want to know where I met him?" she asked me.

I excused myself, because I was laughing so hard. "What's he like?" I asked.

"Don't you want to meet him?" she asked.

"Sure," I answered.

She wanted me to meet him that very day. I guess that when you are eighty-eight, you finally realize that you have no time to waste. He was eighty-four. He was partially blind and living with diabetes. He survived prostate cancer. He had a pacemaker. He was incontinent. His daughter dropped him off in the assisted-living facility after he had kept her household up with his singing in the middle of the night. He was suffering from dementia.

"Sounds like a catch," I said, biting my tongue.

My mother claimed she had fallen in love. They were caught naked in bed one night. They would take their walkers and walk together. He needed her because he could not see well. She needed him because she could not hear well. He drew her pictures and wrote her poems. She taped them on the walls of her room with Scotch tape. They hung askew.

He bought her a plastic necklace at bazaar day in the facility. He asked her to marry him, and she accepted. The facility went along. They tried to convince his daughter and me to pay for a catered affair, a celebration of a union that was never going to be an official marriage, because both my mother and her boyfriend were on Medicaid. My mother planned on keeping her own room after the wedding, which I came to dub "The Walker Wedding That Wasn't." He planned on getting them out of the facility and moving in with my husband and me.

I called him G.I. Joe, because Joe was his nickname, and he had served in the Korean War. G.I. Joe died of a broken heart. He wanted his manhood and independence back so badly. My mother did what she always did best. She survived.

She fell a third time, and this time she broke her pelvis. That did her in, and she ended up in a nursing home. She lasted a year and a half before dying peacefully in her sleep. She was almost ninety-two years old. She had always hated cats. They scared her the way they crept up. But she herself had nine lives.

JEWISH GENEALOGY

I was sixty-two when I first saw a photograph of my maternal grandmother before her hair turned snow white. I guess as a child I always assumed she was born with gray hair. I can remember her yellow parchment face. Her eyes were small and slanted. She was built differently from anyone I knew. She was small boned and short. No one in the family can ever remember her smiling. But it was the shock of thick black hair in a sepia reproduction that my first cousin, my mother's "favorite niece," sent me that made me start to think.

I am tall. I have reddish-brown hair, bright-blue eyes, and a ruddy complexion. In Israel, people mistook me for Irish or Dutch. Growing up here, I looked gentile to the Jewish guys, but as soon as I start talking, there is no mistaking me for anything but Jewish. That is because I am emotional (but clearly not Italian), and I wave my hands around to make sure I am understood.

My father's mother was "Yerushalmi," or born and bred in Jerusalem, and could trace her roots to the Jewish Quarter in the old city going back seven generations. Her second-born son, my uncle, had the same bright-blue eyes and light hair and skin. So did my aunt. My aunt's hair was bright red, and she had the same blue eyes. We three looked Irish. Prior to the genealogy sites on the Internet, I assumed that we three were living proof of the Crusaders, who had brought the Irish to Jerusalem, seeking to restore the Holy Land to Christianity. While they "were working," the Crusaders raped Jewish women. I always kidded that I was a distant product of those rapes. But it was the photograph of my mother's family taken in 1936, when she was fourteen years old, which left me really wondering.

My maternal grandmother's family lives in Israel. I have visited them several times. They look different. They look like her. They are small-boned people with yellowish skin like parchment. They have dark hair and dark slanted eyes. They all look Chinese.

I grew up with a mother who invented truths to serve her needs. She told my cousins and me that we could trace our lineage all the way back to King David himself. She never could provide the proof. I suppose it made her feel better about herself. I never bought her story. I took the photograph and ran to my computer. I looked up the history of Belarus. Minsk...Pinsk...I had heard those names growing up, but my maternal grandmother had been born in the old port city of Jaffa, before Tel Aviv came to be, when it was just sand without a name. No one had really thought about her parents who had fled Russia in the late eighteen hundreds.

The Mongolians invaded Belarus in the twelve hundreds. Waves and waves of Mongolian warriors came through on horseback. They raped the women as they conquered the men. That photograph was living proof that the Mongolians had a direct influence on my family.

When I shared my thoughts with my mother, she was not a believer. Yet in the same breath, she remembered hearing about distant relatives who lived in Chicago.

"Their last name was Chinitz," my mother said slowly and quietly, lost in her memory. "In Yiddish," she added, "Chinitz translates into Chinese people."

I have not yet done the genealogy testing. That is on my still-to-do list. However, now, when Phil starts ticking me off, I say, with total confidence, "Be careful, or that wild Mongolian warrior in me will come out."

It is a warning he does not take lightly.

One year, I was teaching a fifth-grade group of mixed origins about Christopher Columbus. One of the students hailed from Italy. Another was from China. Another was born in the Dominican Republic. I made the story personal. Here was Antonino, who was Christopher Columbus. He wanted to go to Yejin's country of origin, China. Instead, he found himself in the Dominican Republic, where Jocelyn was born.

Jocelyn was a special education student who rarely spoke. I never saw her volunteer any answers. She seemed to doubt anything that came out of her mouth. That day, she raised her hand:

"People are like one big salad," she said.

WHY DIDN'T THEY LET HER SING?

My mother spent her last year wheelchair bound in a nursing facility. She suffered from Parkinson's. Her legs were swollen from edema. Her hands trembled, but her mind was still clear during her last few weeks.

Some of the other patients were catatonic. Some were deaf. Some were depressed. Some had dementia. A new admit joined the floor. She sang. She sang all the time. She drove her roommate crazy with her singing. She sang at lunch. She sang at dinner. I heard her sing "Summertime," and even in her early nineties, she still had a good voice. Her roommate grumbled loudly about the singing.

Her roommate yelled, "Shut up!"

The next time I visited, the woman was not singing. She was telling anyone within earshot about how she used to sing. She used to sing along with the radio. She mentioned Cole Porter, Irving Berlin, and George Gershwin. The next time I visited, she was silent. Her eyes were glazed over. I never heard her voice again.

After lunch that day, the residents stayed to see a performance. Once in a while, the facility brought in entertainment. This afternoon, I watched the aides clean up after lunch and set up for a show in the dining/meeting hall. A bleached-blond woman in her late fifties or early sixties, who was wearing tons of makeup, started singing along with a CD player. She was the entertainment for the month. I looked at the resident singer sitting in her chair. She didn't flinch. She didn't protest. She sat silently with a faraway look. I was not sure she was even watching. Clearly she had been sedated.

Why didn't the facility let that resident sing? She could have entertained the crowd for free after every lunch or before dinner.

Thirty years earlier, I was still freelancing in the arts. I answered an ad to run an arts and crafts project at a Jewish nursing home in Westchester. I packed my car with the supplies. It was a project I had done many times with five-year-olds. I had an hour—just enough time to hand out the trays, the paint, the apples, and allow the residents to print Jewish New Year cards in time for the holiday.

At first, the residents sat around the table listlessly. But as they started working, they came to life. They were laughing and smiling and asked me when I was coming back. It went so well, I was hoping it would turn into a regular gig, but the facility never called me to return. Three years after my experience, *Awakenings*, the movie, came out. A doctor who is hired as a clinical physician at a psychiatric hospital in the Bronx becomes aware that his mostly catatonic patients can respond to certain stimuli. The doctor is granted permission to try an experimental drug on one of the patients. The patient is thus awakened and is very much alive. I understood immediately what had happened. I was a one-night stand. A bunch of feisty ninety-year-olds was too much to handle on a routine basis. Better keep them subdued. Funds are limited. And the people are old.

I know why they really didn't let that resident sing. I once was a substitute teacher in a nursery school, and during free time, all the students were busy. One boy was concentrating on building a tower from blocks. He was hyperfocused and careful. His tower was simple. He meticulously made that column taller and taller. From way across the room, another boy must have spotted the tower rising. Before the head teacher or the aide or I realized what was happening, he tore across and knocked that tower down. The builder dissolved into tears, and the destroyer seemed to win that round.

Institutional settings bring out primal emotions. The residents are easily agitated. Some are so depressed that they do not want to be reminded of the fun that once existed. Cliques arise. Petty jealousies rear their ugly heads. Envy is one of the deadly sins.

After my father died, my mother called to tell me she thought a headstone in the shape of a book would be appropriate for my dad. He revered books and the idea that all human knowledge was written down in books.

"So what will you want as your headstone?" I asked. "Knitting needles?" I remember my mother laughed.

When my mother first went to the nursing home, she was alert enough to know that she was bored. Her body was failing, but her mind was intact. Most of the other long-term residents had failing minds. She had no one with whom she could connect. She wanted something to do. I bought her large-print word search books to do. She did several a day, religiously, to stay keen. She wanted something more. I brought her a bag and filled it with wool. She hung it over the side of her wheelchair. Her arthritic hands shook from Parkinson's, and the medicine no longer masked her trembles. We both knew her knitting days were over. Nonetheless, like a child who clings to a teddy bear and finds comfort, the knitting gear, draped over her wheelchair, seemed to make her feel better about herself.

If my mother were Matisse, would the facility have let her cut shapes with scissors? Matisse did those remarkable works when he was too old to paint. Grandma Moses started painting at seventy.

So why didn't they just let her sing?

CONVERSATION ON THE COUCH

I put the photos of my mother away. I am in my living room, sitting on my couch, looking out of the four large windows opposite me. I can look out at the street and see the passersby, but they cannot see me. I gutted and redid each room one by one. I left the living room for last.

We could have gone on a cruise to Alaska. We could have gone on one of those river cruises in Europe, the kind that are offered in the slick brochures that come almost daily in the mail. Instead, I chose to fix up the living room as a retirement present to myself.

When there are no Amazon delivery boxes lining the floor, and after the recyclables are thrown out, my living room is perfect. The positive space offsets the negative space, and the negative space defines the positive space. Nothing is extraneous, and everything feels balanced. This is my definition of fêng shui.

I love to sit on my couch and let my mind wander. I have put so much of my soul in this space. It is quirky and peaceful, happy and serene. I don't know why, but I only talk to my friend Shelly when I am alone in my living room. I talk to my friend Shelly periodically. She is always available when I need her because she is dead. We used to celebrate our birthdays together at the end of every October, halfway between hers and mine.

"Shelly, I got my Medicare card. See?" And I wave it around.

I don't have to say anything or show her, because if there is an afterlife, she sees, and she knows. And if there isn't, then I am talking to myself. But at my age, it is hard to make new friends.

"Shelly, it happened...A woman friend complimented me on my *outfit* yesterday. I was wearing my chartreuse tunic sweater with the two pockets that I bought in your neighborhood with my black skinny pants. I put on my chartreuse stone necklace with the hand painted pin that I converted into a pendant. Remember we found it at the thrift shop when we were together in Southampton? Well, this woman said, 'Wow, I have never seen a necklace match an outfit so perfectly.'

"Shelly, she did not say, 'Wow *you* look good today.' She was complimenting my outfit—not me! Do you remember your plan to go to Walmart and buy T-shirts and sweats after you retired? Shelly, I am telling you—sorry to say this—you were *wrong*! Your plan would never have worked—not in the city, not in the country, not in Florida. Shelly, one *needs* expensive clothes at this stage in life. I am an Eileen Fisher *small* on top, *medium* on the bottom. Just the labels alone are *priceless*! Cheap clothes simply do not lie right on any sixty-five-year-old body. It is all about the drape, and that drape costs.

"And Shelly—I continue—I *have* to color my hair every four weeks. And because of the melanoma, I am only using organic color. By the way, "organic" does not mean what it used to when we went to Citarella in the Berkshires and got the takeout for Tanglewood. Now "organic" simply means "not genetically modified." Do you remember we forgot a knife and we were starving and Phil ripped that barbecue chicken apart with his bare hands? You would never want to share a bathroom with him! Frankly, neither do I. That is the real reason we are not selling our house and moving to a coop.

"You wanted to retire to your country home near Monticello in the Catskills. I want to retire to a one bedroom coop on the Upper East Side, an apartment like the one you owned. I am tired of the gardening that you so looked forward to doing.

"Remember you talked about selling your Tiffany jewelry? You said you wouldn't need it in the country. The chains must have reminded you of the lifetime of work. Forgive me, Shelly, but I asked for earrings from Tiffany's for my big birthday. I intend to wear those sleek, shiny, dangly earrings every single day and bob my head so that they sway.

"You wanted to go to the club every day, play mahjong, and knit. Shelly, my shoulders, my neck, my upper back all hurt. I discovered that I have no groove in my wrists. So when I pulled my tendon out doing routine exercise, I had to give up the knitting for good.

"You used to go to the gym the way the orthodox go to synagogue. You just wanted to sit by the pool. I never had time to go to the gym. Two hours in the car back and forth every day and a whole day in the classroom drained me. I go to the gym three, four times a week now.

"You hated teaching. You got out after your first year. You became a successful CPA, and you planned to read and read in your retirement. I stuck with the teaching, and in my retirement, I discovered that I love managing my IRA. Now I think I might have become a research analyst in the financial world had I known that women could pursue such a route."

In a hushed voice, I continue:

"Shelly, we danced around the obvious. We never talked about the upheaval in the traditional family roles, about the pressure, the stress, the burden of supporting husbands who had once been successful. Both their first wives never thought they had to work. We found our men after they were pushed out in a wave of mergers and acquisitions in a rapidly shrinking industry. We became the primary breadwinners. You developed lupus trying to keep it all in. I raged and ranted inside my four walls. We kept our honest, raw, and ugly feelings to ourselves, and we continued to support our good men because they really were good men who had just lost out. But the responsibility of carrying another adult was immense and took its toll. The resentment crept into the tone of our voices, and when it did, we shied away from it. Instead, we talked about cooking and step-grandchildren and our cats. We were women who wanted to be women and did not want to become men. Our men wanted to be men, but neither of them was able to successfully replace the career he chose in his twenties, a career that was supposed to last way beyond his early forties. There, Shelly, I just ranted and raved for both of us. I feel better. I hope you do, too!"

The doorbell rings. "Hold that thought," I say, running to answer the front door.

AMAZON PRIME

Another Amazon Prime package was just delivered. I cannot fathom what is inside. I wanted to purchase Amazon stock three years ago, but my friends talked me out of it. Amazon was losing money. How could they be losing money? I was probably supporting them all by myself. I keep shaking my head. At the rate I am going, Amazon should be offering me *stock* instead of reward points.

I am addicted to Amazon Prime because I do not want to spend time sitting in traffic anymore. I commuted two hours a day. I did the math, and I spent *eleven thousand* hours behind the wheel. That is the equivalent of one extra week per month for twenty-five years, or a total of *over five years* of my life!

Usually the items in the boxes are enrichment toys or educational books that I buy for my grandchildren. But clearly, this box is way too big. When I take out the packing material, I see what I purchased just two days before. There they are—the six lumbar-support pillows. We do need the additional support, but these stick out like sore thumbs. *Old people live here*, they scream. I will give them to my next-door neighbor as a present. She is in her nineties, and she and her sisters will appreciate them. There is old, and then there is *old*, I decide. I will have to have custom lumbar-support pillows made so that they look decorative rather than utilitarian. That means that I will have to spend additional money in order to make a product for the aging look like an upscale product for the middle-aged, active people we imagine ourselves to be. I already spent money on slipcovers, not the plastic ones my mother used to have. When the first grandchild began to toddle, I realized that my Ethan Allen chairs needed protection. I was smarter than I was when my daughter was little. I knew what to expect. I knew how to anticipate. I had really cool custom slipcovers made. They actually add to the shabby chic look of the beach cottage and match the cornices brilliantly. No one can possibly call these old lady slipcovers. I look upward.

"See, Shelly? I told you, and it is not only the clothes that have to drape just so."

When we needed a new mattress, we found ourselves trying Sleep Number Beds. We ordered the adjustable one. We thought we were so cool. We press a remote control, and the back goes up. We press another setting and legs lift. The bed arrived with the pump, and all we thought about were hospital beds. We remembered the commercials for the Craftmatic bed, the original adjustable bed, *the* bed for old people. Now when we go to sleep, we ask ourselves: What happened to the Clapper? Clap on, clap off; lights on, lights off.

"Oh, Shelly," I say as I look around my house. "Do you remember what this house used to look like?"

At the time, our house was the cheapest one in the best neighborhood that we could afford. My husband ascribes to Warren Buffet's approach to purchasing real estate. Warren Buffet ascribes to buying an affordable home, not a dream home. When we purchased this home, it was more of a nightmare house. It was an original beach cottage on the North Shore of Long Island and had once serviced a middle-class family from Queens as their summer home. It was built almost a century ago. If fifty years old qualifies as antique, then the house and the two of us are all antiques. Aren't antiques priceless? The house was small. It was dark. It had brown Formica and layers of linoleum. It made me feel poor, and I hate feeling poor. Tears started flowing down my cheeks. I sat down on the living-room floor and sobbed. Phil sat down next to me and wrapped his arms around me.

"What's wrong?" he asked gently.

"It's so small," I muttered. "It's so ugly. What am I going to do with this?"

Phil was silent for a while. Then he said, "It's a beach cottage. Why not just make it a beach cottage?"

And the tears turned, just like that, into smiles. At Phil's suggestion, nay, at his insistence, we got in the car and drove directly to the library. We found a stack of decorating and design magazines that showcased beach cottages. It turns out that, just as we were starting over again from scratch, others were onto their second-home getaways, and beach cottages everywhere were in vogue.

In one of the magazines, I found a picture of a small beach cottage with casement windows that looked like ours. They were covered with bleached-wood shutters, and they were unmistakably the look I was going for. I called the designer who was listed in the source department at the back of the magazine. He was from Seattle, and the cute beach condo was on one of the islands off the West Coast. Since I was in New York and he was there, he kindly offered a suggestion at no charge. He told me that there was no need to have custom shutters made: if I would just order bleached-wood mini blinds, I could achieve the look without the cost. Phil wasted no time. It was the recessionary 1990s, and barter was still in its heyday. Phil traded advertising space for seven wooden blinds. Three would cover the windows in the dining area; four would cover the ones in the living area. They would anchor the living area, and they would be my compass, my north star. Everything I did from then on, I did with purpose. I had a theme and all I had to do was work that theme.

The blinds arrived ten days later, and my Phil began hanging the blinds one at a time that very day.

From time to time, Phil reminds me that Julius Caesar's mother had been able to support her children by renting out apartments in a building her family owned. Evidently, Julius Caesar's father died, and his mother's family wanted to make sure that no matter what happened, Caesar's mother would have a steady source of income. Phil insists we hold onto our little house because he knows that I am concerned about the future. Will Social Security exist for my daughter? Will she be able to save enough for her retirement? Phil always knew and still knows that the way to *this* woman's heart is through her child. Phil wants my daughter to inherit the house and rent it out so that I will not have to worry from beyond as to how she is getting by. I simply have no choice. I *have* to love him. I am about to remind him that Shelly used to say Jewish people do not invest in real estate. We invest in diamonds because they are portable. But then I remember that Shelly herself owned two pieces of real estate.

Another package arrives. I remember once, Amazon delivered during a bad snowstorm. The district closed the schools. The newscasters asked people to stay inside. The media announced that the roads were virtually impassable. Then the doorbell rang, and an Amazon Prime package got to me on time. My mind was wandering, and I saw that Phil was getting annoyed.

"What did you buy now?" he demands to know, and I cannot supply the answer.

I open the box, and to my surprise, I pull out a bright-hot-pink scarf. Oh, yes, I remember that I did order that one to go with my bright yellow-green long shirt. I look upward and silently tell Shelly that in your sixties, a woman simply *must* have scarves. Colorful scarves that go around one's neck and hide that unsightly skin sag and help distract from the washed-out, beaten-up, faded look that shows through even under all the creams and makeup. Colorful scarves that divert attention away from your floppy neck and the tired look in your eyes that tell everyone you are past your prime and are now, officially, on the maintenance plan.

THE MAINTENANCE PLAN

S omeone in the 1 percent was quoted as saying, "It is easy to make money. It is a lot harder to maintain it." Maintenance for me feels like the kiss of death. It means I am no longer innovating. It means I am spending all my time and energy and money just trying to hold on.

I am trying to maintain my health. I never knew we had so many body parts. I never knew there were so many doctors. More than half the contacts I have in all my devices are under the letter *D* for doctor. There is the allergist, audiologist, and acupuncturist; the breast specialist; the chiropractor and cardiologist; the dentist and dermatologist; the endocrinologist and ENT specialist; the jaw specialist for TMJ; Lab Corp; the mental health specialist a.k.a. the therapist; the neurologist; the orthopedist, opthalmologist and oncologist; the physical therapist, pulmonologist, pharmacist, and podiatrist, a.k.a. the foot specialist; Quest Lab; the radiologist for mammograms and sonograms; the therapist a.k.a the mental health specialist; the urologist; the visiting nurse for when we come home from surgery and the veterinarian for if

I get another kitten to replace my Tigger; the x-ray technicians for plain old x-rays. Have I left anyone out? Each one is a specialist. But I am one whole person, and no one seems to know it. The podiatrist is not the back doctor. Yet, because of my feet, I have poor posture. The hand doctor is not the neurologist. Yet I have tingles and numbness in my fingers. Is it a pinched nerve in my back? Is it carpal tunnel syndrome? The cancer specialist is not the cardiologist. Who will approve of the herbal supplement that I have decided to take to ward off melanoma from returning? Who is running this job? I cannot be my own general contractor! And so far, we have not found that elusive general practitioner, who would get filed under the letter *G*.

My husband and I share some doctors but not all, so I have all his doctors in my contact list as well. Phil has given each and every one of them permission to talk to me on his behalf. Of course he did! He knows that I am on top of everything. Onto my husband's health: I keep trying to maintain his health. I had him start taking saw palmetto in his forties to ward off prostate cancer. I have him on CoQ10 to help ward off whatever it is supposed to ward off. I make sure he goes to his doctors regularly. He is older than I am, and so he has more things wrong with him. Yet he is stronger than I am. I remind him to take his morning meds. I remind him to take his nighttime meds. I am desperate to maintain his health because I desperately do not want to be alone.

Every month, we have at least one doctor's appointment between us. Sometimes we have two or three. Sometimes we have three or four doctor appointments in one week. Dental and eye doctor appointments are add-ons. You have to go through the robo systems to get an appointment. You have to wait to see the doctor. Then you have to go to the pharmacist and drop off the prescription(s). Then you have to go back to pick them up. Then you have to set your follow-up appointment. This is what I mean by maintenance. It is tedious and constant and time-consuming.

MY KITCHEN

My kitchen is literally the hub of my house. It is smack in the middle, and you have to walk through it to get from the front of the house to the back of the house. It was a small beach cottage, after all. It is here that I do most of the physical work. I have five mugs filled with scissors, highlighters, pens, pencils, glue sticks, scotch tape, and rulers. They are sitting on one kitchen countertop, and they take up a lot of space. Recently, I discovered that my fingers do not work as dexterously as I thought I remembered. Every order from Amazon is packaged so well that I have trouble opening what I bought. But it is not only the packages that I have difficulty with. The medicine bottles are sometimes virtually impossible to open. These hands that drew so many drawings, painted so many paintings, made so many collages, planted so many flowers, pulled so many weeds—these fingers that knitted so many afghans, scarves, and shawls—simply do not work the way they used to.

Phil was always strong, but he was never delicate. The older he gets, the clumsier he gets. So now that I finally have the jewelry I want, I can no longer manage the clasps, and he cannot manage those clasps either. Those clasps have become too delicate for him to open and close. So I sit at the kitchen counter, with all the lights turned on, and like King Midas, I lovingly touch my jewelry as I put on my reading glasses to view my pieces. Maybe the problem is that the stones aren't big enough. Maybe the problem is that the chains aren't bulky enough.

The other countertop is full of gadgets and appliances. Prominently on display is a jar-opener contraption because all those thick rubber bands still require wristwork, and our wrists do not grip and twist the way they used to. There is the electric can opener, the toaster, the George Forman grill, the blender, the electric coffeemaker, the electric teapot, and the food processor. All these mini appliances are too heavy and/or too cumbersome to keep taking out and putting away. How will we ever stage the kitchen if and when we decide to move?

We might be able to store unsightly stuff up in our attic, but the adult children have taken over that space to store all their stuff that is still wanted but that they have no room for. They are storing boxes and boxes of stuff until they buy a house. Which will come sooner: our decision to move to an apartment or their decision to move to a house?

"ADULT CHILDREN" IS AN OXYMORON

Children are a fabulous distraction. From the exact moment they arrive, they do not care about your own unresolved issues. They need what they need, and they want what they want so that they can grow. You cannot look back or over your shoulder to try to fix what might have been broken in your own childhood. You have to focus on your children. You have to do your job and be the parent, even if you are unprepared, not trained, or ill-equipped.

"Adult children" has to be an oxymoron. And it is confusing... very confusing. A young colleague of mine once joked that her mother would still be breastfeeding her if she could.

Sometimes I think we have children in order to have grandchildren. The only part of *The Good Earth*, by Pearl S. Buck, that still stands out for me, fifty-two years after reading the book, is the part where the little boy's job was to sleep in his grandfather's bed in order to warm his grandfather's old bones at night. I need my grandchildren to warm my heart.

My favorite commercial was the one in which a young mother is holding her cell and calling her mother. She asks about the house across the street from her mom: "Is it still for sale?" Her mother looks out, sees the SOLD sign, and tells her daughter. "I know," her daughter says as she walks out of this very house, thus announcing that she bought the house across the street from her mom. *Please* do not ask me what the commercial is for. It could be for a Realtor. It could be for a cell phone. It could be for a moving company. I don't remember what I had for breakfast. But that has become my favorite commercial ever since my cousin's daughter moved into an apartment in the same condo building as my cousin. Now when the oldest grandchild gets dropped off from school, he can go directly to his grandparents, and his mom can continue to work for the rest of the day without worrying about what will happen if she runs late. I remember how hard it was to be a single mom, raise a daughter, and work two jobs. I retired hoping I could make my daughter's life easier.

I wanted my daughter to be independent but not too independent (like the time she drove herself across the country and was living in San Francisco, and I was miserable). I wanted my daughter to explore and experience the world, but I wanted my daughter to live nearby. I cupped her face and told her that we were not rich enough to be bicoastal. I wanted my daughter to be able to support herself, but I also wanted her to need my help (I told my daughter I could help her if she lived closer). I wanted my daughter to be successful, but I also wanted her to share details. (I would love for her to call me every day and tell me about her job and her children— never mind that she has no time to breathe.) I wanted her to think for herself, but I also wanted her to follow our traditions. I wanted her to be part of the big world, but I wanted her to stay close to her roots. I wanted her to forge a close and intimate relationship with her husband, but I also wanted her to call me and share every special moment. I have one daughter, and I want it all from her.

It is tricky. I love to shower my adult child with things I never had, with support I needed but never received. However, I do not want to smother her. I do not want her to conclude that I do not believe in her. I do not want her to feel that I do not trust her judgment. Yet it gives me pleasure to help. I want to be part of my adult child's life. (I have so much more experience; she is working, and I have more free time.) However, when I do help, I do not want to feel that my adult child is taking advantage of me. I do not want to feel used or abused or taken for granted. Also, I certainly do not want to feel that I *am* the Amazon fulfillment center or "the help." I want to be cherished for giving, but I do not only want to give on her terms.

Only a mother who has worked full time knows the trials and tribulations of another working mom. So every time I call my daughter, I ask her if there is anything we can do to help. I make suggestions, such as "I can cook for you," "We are willing to babysit on Saturday evening," "I am willing to fold laundry when we come over." Things like that. Every time she asks for help, we try very hard to oblige. Every time we offer, she tells us she is good. That is how I know that my almost middle-aged daughter is not yet mature. When you are truly mature, you simply cannot believe that anyone else is actually *offering* help, and you do not hesitate. "*Yes!*" should just pop out of your mouth and you should feel such relief and gratitude.

I have held this theory in my head for a long, long time. You take the average life-span and divide it in half. The first half you are just growing up, and the second half you are an adult. Since our life-span is currently into our nineties, we cannot expect our "adult children" to really be mature until they are forty-five or even fifty!

A friend of mine answered yes when I asked if we are trying to buy our children's love. I found his answer to be refreshingly honest. I felt happy; thank goodness we can afford to buy a piece of our children's love, and thank goodness we cannot afford to buy all their love!

DAILY LIFE: IT'S ALL IN THE DETAILS

It is time to get dressed, because we are going out this evening. When I want to look my very best, I start getting ready at ten o'clock in the morning. I put in a second bathroom a few years ago. Maybe it is more than a few years ago, but when you are sixty, even fifteen years feels like just a few years ago. We only had four feet by six feet of unused space. I had trained as a space planner in the time I could not find a teaching job, and before the design field collapsed. I created a fabulous little bathroom with porcelain tiles on the floor and shower. I added a skylight so that I could see the trees and sky while showering. I drew from my friends' outdoor shower at their beach cabana. I drew from the Roman bath artifacts that I saw outside Jerusalem. It is compact but elegant. And that is *my* bathroom. I rarely enter my husband's bathroom, because when I do, I am quickly reminded that Phil was, and still is, a frat boy. His bathroom needs to be upgraded again, but there is leftover water on the counter that is dripping to the floor. The towels are wet. The toilet is not always flushed, and there is gook in the sink.

At Pratt, where I studied art and design, we were taught that it is all about the details. Sure, form followed function, but the craft was in the details. It wasn't about *what* you did but *how* you did it. Now that I am retired, I have time to study the details. And those details are *overwhelming*. I am trying to maintain our money. I am trying to make it last. How do I make it last if I have to maintain everything all at the same time? Do I really want to have the house painted, or do I want to take a trip?

We have each made bucket lists, but we keep adding to them so the bucket is never full. There is always someplace new that pops up.

And so we keep working part time.

"Until we reach diminishing returns," my husband keeps saying.

Well, yes, it is really all about diminishing returns. The trick to aging, I think, is being able to recognize when you get to diminishing returns. That is not as easy as it may seem because that means giving up, letting go. How do I prioritize? What do I let go of and when? Isn't letting go really a sign of accepting defeat? I pride myself on having made it against the odds. My husband prides himself on having a work ethic. My girlfriend constantly reminds me that there is no rest for the weary.

Evidently, even the famous painter Bonnard suffered from not being able to let go. When I studied art, a professor told us that Bonnard was caught by a security guard touching up one of his own paintings even as it hung in the museum. The guard then escorted Bonnard out of the museum, his paintbrushes and oil paints in hand.

The maintenance plan continues. While I was working full time, I was too busy to notice that not just *everyone* but also *everything* needs *constant* maintenance.

The mailman comes and shakes me out of my reverie. There is a pile of mail—mostly catalogs, some junk mail, and a few bills. I once took a class in ID-theft protection, and I am proud to say that I got the highest score. Personally, I think it is smart to be paranoid. I do not just sort my mail. I open all the mail, tear off our name and address wherever they appear, and shred that information. My daughter tells me that will not protect me against Internet hacking, which is the most common form of identity theft. But I do what I can to protect myself. That adds to the amount of time I spend doing this mundane task. What should take three minutes can take me half an hour, depending on what time of year it is; the closer to a holiday, the more the volume, and the more time I spend tearing and shredding.

On my to-do list are the following: Call the insurance companies. Call Medicare. Call the secondary health-insurance company. Call the supplemental-insurance company. They all require periodic phone calls. There is the robo call; then the representative; then going through the security questions; then my question; and then, hopefully, the answer. This is what I mean by maintenance. It is repetitive. There is a lot of wait time. It takes time and diligence. It wears me down. Life should be more interesting than waiting on hold.

I am trying to maintain our money. I am trying to make it last. So how do I make it last if I have to maintain everything all at the same time?

There is the house, our so-called greatest asset, but also our greatest money pit. I am afraid that if I do not maintain my house, one day I will wake up in an old lady's house, and that old lady will be me. Then I worry that I may not wake up at all.

I am trying to maintain my looks the best I can. There is the hair stylist, the colorist, the manicurist, and the pedicurist. There is the threader, because now that my hair is thinning everywhere I want it, I am finding unwanted hair growing in places I never knew it could! There is the trainer because I was sedentary for too many years.

There are the daily rituals, the facial cleansers and the toners, the balance serums and the moisturizing creams, because wrinkles have no mercy.

Smoke detectors need their batteries changed every year. The carbon monoxide detectors, the devices themselves, need to be replaced every five years. Who can keep track of all this?

We need to eat, which means the dishes and pots and pans need to be washed. Then they need to be put away. We have to go food shopping. We have to load the bags into the car and unload them when we get home. We have to put all the food away—in the fridge, in the pantry.

Laundry has to be washed, dried, folded or hung, and put away. We have to drop off and pick up the dry cleaning.

I find that all these tedious chores take more and more time for me to do. In fact, I am exhausted just thinking about them.

This is what I mean by maintenance. How did I ever work? I *am* a full-time job!

In my late fifties, I was still multitasking at work and at home. My kitchen is, literally, in the middle of my house. The stackable washer-dryer is on the other side of the wall. I used to cook, roast, run the dishwasher, throw a load in the washer, dry a load in the dryer, turn on the coffee machine, and boil water in the electric tea kettle—all simultaneously. I was master of doing it all and all at once.

But then *it* happened. I was running a load in the washer, and I decided that I wanted a cup of herbal tea. I heard the noise of water and poured myself a cup. But the tea in the teabag was still intact, and the water was cold. My first thought was that the kettle was broken. I turned it over to see where it was made. Then I heard the noise again. I could not identify it at first, but as I turned around, I realized it was my washing machine. I had never even plugged the tea kettle in. Clearly, I can only do *one* machine at a time now!

When I first went back to teaching, my principal was busy signing a piece of paper when I barged in to tell him something that

I thought important. He looked up and asked me to wait and explained, politely, that he could only do one thing at a time. I chuckled inside. Tell that to the business world I came from, I laughed to myself. I had been a high-powered go-getter in the commercial design field before the recession of the early 1990s set in, before all the creative industries in Manhattan got squished, before I understood just how precarious the business world really is and how long a recession can last if you are directly affected.

Now, I do one task at a time and only one a day. If I go shopping, I do not cook. If I cook, I do not wash the clothes. If I wash the clothes, I do not fold and put them away the same day. Each task requires one day.

It is true that Phil participates in most of the chores. But it is also true that I have to remind him, nudge him, coax him, ask him, and show him. He reminds me of a student I once had. Brian was in first grade. I was a pull-out teacher who serviced English language learners. Brian had just figured out how to read.

"Let's show your classroom teacher how you read," I said excitedly. I still get a thrill when a child breaks the code and starts reading.

Brian slowed down. "Come on, Brian." I was practically skipping.

Brian walked reluctantly. "Brian, what's the matter? Mrs. Kapps will be so proud of you!" I said.

Brian stopped walking. "What's the matter? What's wrong?" I asked.

"Don't tell her. Please don't tell her," Brian whispered.

"Why? Why not?" I asked.

"Because if she knows, she will make me do more work," Brian explained.

I thought then, and I think now, who is smarter: the one who gives his all, all the time? Or the one who realizes they just load it on you if you do?

MY BIGGEST PET PEEVE

Ask any middle-aged woman about the movie *Fried Green Tomatoes,* and a smile will flash across her face. Kathy Bates's character was dismissed and insulted by two provocative young women. She looks beaten down. She looks all washed up. But slowly, the audience can see her come to life. The outrage that she feels and the revenge she takes have to be fresh on any middle-aged woman's mind, as Kathy Bates's character repeatedly rams her car into the young woman's sporty coupe parked in the parking lot, because of her age. "I'm older, and I have more insurance!"

I do not have it in for young women, but I do have it in for the survey callers. It is nothing personal. Before the survey callers, I had it in for the telemarketers who used to call often, especially around dinnertime. That was before caller ID. As soon as I heard that foreign accent, I would get all supersweet. "Where are you calling from?" I would ask. That was not in their script, and it threw them off. "Are you in India or Pakistan?" I would continue, because in those days almost all the outsourced calling centers were located in those two countries. "What is the weather like?" I continued. Then when they started their sales pitch, I would simply say, "No, thank you," and hang up.

But now, we have a national disease on our hands. It can be my bank or brokerage firm. It can be any store where I bought an appliance or have an extended warranty. It can be my computer server or my phone carrier. It can be my health-insurance provider. I call to ask *one* question, and I get a follow-up survey call in return. Sometimes, the survey call is followed up by a postsurvey call about the survey call. This is what actually happened: I entered a wrong password. I reentered the wrong password, and I got locked out of my account. Obviously, I needed to call and get help.

The representative helped me, and I did not have to reset my password. The next evening, I got a call from the brokerage firm. I thought maybe they were selling a product that I might be interested in. The stock market is up, then down, then up a little. Maybe I will learn something, I thought.

It was a follow-up survey phone call to the call I had made the previous day. "How satisfied are you with the way the representative handled the situation?" the woman asked.

"I'm sorry," I said, and I was. I was sorry that I picked up the phone. "I do not understand your question."

She repeated the question, a little slower, the way you do if you think someone is hard of hearing or speaks a different language.

"No," I repeated. "I don't understand. How satisfied was I with the way the representative handled the situation? He answered my question," I explained.

"On a scale of one to ten, with one being completely dissatisfied and ten being extremely satisfied, how satisfied were you with the way the representative handled the situation?"

"Well," I began thinking out loud, "he answered my question. I was satisfied that he answered the question."

"So satisfied, very satisfied, or extremely satisfied?" she asked.

A good meal came to mind. "He answered my question, so I was definitely satisfied," I said, ready to hang up.

She continued to ask me a second question that sounded almost identical to the original question. I was getting confused. "I do not understand this question," I said, honestly flustered. "Stop," I said. "He did *not* invite me to dinner. He did *not* make the stock market jump one thousand points. The representative did his job. I asked one question, and he answered it. Now you are asking me *two* questions about one question. How many questions are on this survey?"

"Just a few more," she said, trying to coax me.

"Wait," I said, "The representative was doing his job. If he didn't answer the question, then he should not have this job. But he did his job. Isn't the rep working for a paycheck? And if he isn't, then why is he receiving one? I don't get it."

The following day, I had a routine sonogram scheduled. The technician was chitchatting, trying to make me feel more at ease. She complained that her boyfriend, who worked for an insurance company, did not get his bonus because he was rated *only* satisfactory on his performance. And that performance was based upon the survey calls that were made and the responses given.

I began to sweat. Maybe the rep from my brokerage firm has a wife and kids. Maybe the bonus money is not extra money. Maybe he needs it to pay the babysitter.

The first thing I remember doing was calling back the brokerage company. I had to explain. I did not want my negative comments to reflect upon the person who was kind enough to answer my question. I was transferred to a supervisor. I explained that I had no complaint with the person who had handled my situation and helped me. I had a gripe with the wording of the questions in the survey.

"I mean, the choice between *satisfied, very satisfied*, and *extremely satisfied*. When I think of extremely satisfied, I think of a fabulously

expensive dinner in New York City. That would be *extremely* satisfying. I might even think of extraordinary sex. That would be *extremely* satisfying. Do you see what I mean?" I asked the supervisor.
"So I think it would be *extreme* on my part to be *extremely* satisfied
with a person who just did his job and answered my one question.
If I answer that I am extremely satisfied, then I would have to come
up with another word to describe an exquisite dinner, or mad,
hot passionate sex. But since this guy's bonus may depend on my
answers and my *extreme* satisfaction, please fill in that I was *orgasmi-
cally* satisfied for every one of your questions!"

FORGETTING AND REMEMBERING

I seem to have replaced my two-hour-a-day commute with a two-hour-a-day traipse through the house trying to find something I have misplaced. I did not need reading glasses until recently. Now I don't need glasses for distance anymore except for the fact that I have an astigmatism. I have a pair of progressive lenses that are great for driving. However, they annoy me when I am in the house reading. I prefer my prescription reading glasses. I devised a system that is meant to work. I am supposed to simply leave my driving glasses in the car. However, I forget anything on the periphery, and inevitably, I wear those glasses into the house after I have been out and about. And so I keep spending hours a week looking for either my driving-reading glasses or my plain reading glasses. In addition, I have prescription sunglasses. Sometimes I wear them when I have to drive. Often I forget to take them off and wear them in. Thus, the three-ring circus continues. This has become an everyday annoyance. It never fails. I cannot find the right pair of glasses when I need them, which is, really, all the time.

There were many times I could not find my cell phone. I would call my cell from my home phone. I began to notice that I could not find my cell phone on more and more occasions. Now I find myself calling my own cell phone all the time. I don't know whether that is because I discovered a shortcut that actually works or because I cannot find my phone even when I know for sure it is in my bag.

Every morning I ask the same question: "Did I or did I not take my morning meds?" I have always had issues with my short-term memory. Anything on the periphery drops by the wayside. Unless I focus and pay 100 percent attention to what I am doing and actually say out loud that I have done something, mechanical actions do not register, and I do not remember whether or not I have actually done them. This forces me to go back and check the heating setting, the a/c setting, the electric heater, the coffeemaker, the windows, the oven, the range, the back door, the front door.

I replaced the time of my commute with checking and double-checking myself ever since I left my oven turned to 350 degrees with roasting chicken breasts in it. We went to the gym. We met a friend. We went out to grab a bite, and five hours after we left the house, in the middle of a sentence, I screamed, "We have to go home!"

I called the fire department from the car, and they said they would meet us at the house. Phil still did not believe me until we smelled my chicken halfway down the block. The house was still standing, and there were no black plumes of smoke. The firemen took Phil's house keys and told us to stand back as they went inside. They laughed and told us we had a great oven. The chicken breasts were dry, but they were not burned. I do not think it was the oven. I think it was my recipe. I marinated the chicken breasts in Italian dressing and then coated them with crushed cornflakes. The dressing makes the chicken juicy, which makes them extra delicious. The corn flakes keep the moisture locked in so they come out really tender, unless they are overcooked…

I fret when I forget important things. I have a reputation for being meticulous, responsible, reliable, OCD, anal, and a perfectionist. Phil did not believe me until he saw for himself. And if I, indeed, remembered that I had left the oven on, do I really have a memory issue?

Maybe I would worry less if that was the *only time* I had forgotten to shut the oven off. But it was not. Something similar happened again. I warmed up delicious flounder fillets that I prepared that morning. I turned the oven on, and when the fish was hot, I served dinner. *Six hours later*, as I was getting ready for bed, I went to turn out the light in the kitchen. Heat seemed to be emanating from the stove. I checked it, and sure enough, it was still on the 325-degree setting. I could have made a whole Thanksgiving feast in the hours I had accidentally left that oven on.

"Didn't my friend Renee place her dad in a facility after he left the range on?" I ask Phil. "I am not what I used to be," I tell Phil.

"Neither am I," he answers.

"*Oy vey!*" I continue. "How does one know when it is time to go into assisted living?"

"Remember what Renee told us? Her father used to say, 'Make your habits work for you.'" Phil explains, "Her father would put a towel on the floor when he turned the range on. Then when he saw the towel on the floor, he would ask himself what the towel was doing there, and then he would remember that he put it there so that he could not forget to check the range and turn it off. He could not live alone only when he was well into his nineties and could no longer see the towel on the floor. That is why he left the range on, and that is how Renee knew it was time."

Last January, the weather turned cold and snowy. The snow turned to ice and the ice lasted and lasted. We stopped going to the gym on a routine basis. The sky seemed to remain gray for weeks. Then, on a beautiful day in the early spring, I coaxed Phil into going back to the gym. It was time to stop hibernating. I fiddled with the locker-room lock in my hand. I could not remember the combination. I tried two different ways and got it open on my third try!

"So I am *not* senile after all," I announced triumphantly.

"You should have written the numbers down," Phil chided me.

And then I remembered. I had, indeed, written the combination down—in my cell phone, so that I would *never* have to worry about forgetting it…

"What counts more," I ask myself, "what I remember or what I forget?"

And how is it that I remember what I forgot?

STRETCHING AND
KVETCHING

In decent weather, I find myself hanging out at the gym a lot. For someone as sedentary as I used to be, I am discovering a whole new side to me, and isn't that exactly what you have to do to stay fresh and vital? I try to exercise six hours a week. I am actually happy after I force myself to do forty-five minutes of cardio and an additional fifteen minutes of weight training. I even joined a class once a week.

I have to force Phil to join me. He was athletic all his life, and suddenly, in his retirement, he prefers his books and audiobooks. Phil grew up amid the cornfields of Dayton, Ohio. He thrived on structure. During the week, he went to school, and on the weekends, he played competitive sports. He thrived on winning. He took every game seriously.

In his twenties, way before I knew him, Phil left Ohio to come to New York City. He was accepted at New York University to do a master's in history in the evening while he fulfilled his dream of becoming a "MadMan" during the day. Phil worked in the creative departments of famous agencies, won prestigious awards, and fulfilled his football dream playing on the weekends in Central Park. In his forties, Phil began to coach the softball games for his company in the corporate after-work leagues. But he can no longer play team sports. Now, he has to watch sports to get the vicarious thrill of winning.

After his career in advertising ended, he tried to go back to New York University to finish his master's thesis. He wanted to write about the Blue Eagle campaign, when labor and management both got behind the National Recovery Act to try to pull out of the Great Depression. This was Roosevelt's first attempt. After thirty years and his own economic depression, Phil finally realized that FDR kept using trial and error as his modus operandi until the Rearmament of the Allies finally provided the employment that was necessary to facilitate the recovery. However, forty years had gone by, and it was too late for Phil to reregister. Nonetheless, his passion for history did not die, and he began to listen to the Superstar Teachers Series on history. He is a voracious audiobook "reader." He rediscovered the public library, which was his favorite weekday hangout as a kid. He reinvented himself. He taught history and English in private schools. He created a program he dubbed "From Moses to Mel Brooks," a tribute to the Jewish greats in Hollywood. He rediscovered his roots.

I took a water aerobics class once a week when I was working. Going to the pool made me feel like I was on vacation. I used to imagine myself in the Caribbean. Why didn't they decorate the pool deck with palm trees? When our instructor, a former Czech Olympics bronze medalist, was going on vacation, I asked her if she was going to a beach. She replied curtly:

"I never go near the water when I am on vacation. That would be work."

The first thing I do when I am on vacation is to take off my watch. I used to be on such a tight schedule that I had to set my watch ten minutes ahead so that I would be on time wherever I had to be. We book our vacations at a beach. The first thing I do after we go up to our room is book myself in for a spa treatment or two: a massage, a facial, a mani-pedi. I never pack a book, never pick up a pen or pencil. I swim or collect seashells. I sit and stare at the water. I never mingle. I empty my brain. I take in my fill of nature. I breathe. I listen to the lapping of the waves, the coqui frogs, the birds.

From time to time, I book in for a massage at one of our local day spas. I imagine that I am on a minivacation when I lie down and breathe in the scented mist. I became friendly with the owner of the spa. She mentioned that she was going on vacation.

"Do you get a massage?" I asked her.

"No way," she replied. "I sit in a hammock and read all day long. I love to read."

Who knew?

After we bought our little cottage, I became an avid gardener. Every spring, I would stop in at one of our local nurseries and purchase a few perennials to add to my garden. One day, on a whim, I asked the owner what kinds of flowers he has in his garden. I was hoping to get a few new ideas. To my surprise, he blurted out, "I don't have any flowers in my garden. They are too much work."

I spent my youth and young adulthood reading books. I lived through books. I discovered my own feelings through books. Now *all* I want to do is exercise, move my body, feel my heart beat, and sweat. My class is full of older women. We stretch and *kvetch*. As I stretch, I am aware that I am stretching more than my body. I am reaching for something that I cannot yet name.

In the meantime, we *kvetch* and stretch. That one has a bum knee. The other one has obvious problems with her heels. I have eight hammertoes. Another one broke her hip and is trying to get her strength back. That one has a bad lower back. I may not know the women's names, but I know what parts of their bodies are giving them trouble.

I am in awe of the athletes who bow out of their careers in sports when they are just at the height of their skill. They know to leave before they begin their decline. But aging is more complicated. No one wants to bow out of life, not until it is unbearable. So the lesson is that I must reinvent myself yet again. Perhaps modeling myself on a snake that sheds its skin when it needs to move on is a more appropriate model for me.

I exercise religiously. I babysit my grandkids. I cook healthy meals. I tutor. I write. I cannot sit around and wait for my end. I cannot drink myself to death while watching TV. I must stay fresh. I thrive on challenge. I love projects, and I realize, the truth is, I love to work. Not for others—I love to work for myself. Aging in a graceful, meaningful way feels like a daunting task, but I am determined to be an appropriate role model for my daughter, so that she, in turn, will be an appropriate role model for my granddaughter.

A LOT OF STUFF

P hil grew up collecting. His father served in World War II, and
when he came back, he started collecting stamps. Then he
started collecting coins. He taught Phil about collecting coins, and
together they bought and saved. My mother worked in an import-
export business after she quit high school to help provide her
family with money. She became smitten with stamp collecting. My
mother tried to interest me in her hobby, but I never understood it.
My mother died believing that her collection was worth way more
than the $250 that a collector offered her, and that I told her to
take, but she refused. When it came time for Phil to go to college,
Phil's coin collection paid his tuition.

Phil and his brother also grew up collecting baseball cards and
autographs. They belonged to a club and wrote a letter once a
month and waited for baseball players to send them their autographs on simple index cards.

Phil used to go to estate sales in Connecticut where he was
living, and I used to go to estate sales on Long Island where I was
living. We were both married to our first spouses and did not know

each other, but we shared this hobby. I was trying to decorate for cheap, and Phil was continuing his hobby of buying collectibles at cheap prices and selling them off piecemeal at higher prices. We were both into supplemental income.

When we met, we both had vintage pieces. Phil came with an antique trunk that was held together with handmade nails from the 1800s. I came with a pair of lamps my mother had inherited as hand-me-downs in the 1930s. I came with a silver bowl I bought at a thrift shop. Phil came with half of his sterling silverware. We later sold the silverware to a collector.

Collectors are odd people. They like to talk and swap stories. I was sure that after an hour of circuitous conversation, the collector was just a lonely woman looking for company. But a full hour and a half brought the deal to a close, and we had some extra cash in our hands. I came with two oriental carpets and a 1920s dresser. Phil came with an antique card table that served as our dining table. I came with a hand-me-down sofa. Phil came with a coffee table. I came with a stereo, and Phil came with a working TV. I came with everyday dishes, and he came with everyday drinking glasses. It was a match made in heaven.

When Phil's advertising business was slow, he would do what he learned to do in his childhood. He sold his various collectibles. He paid our mortgage for a whole year by selling off his baseball cards at weekend shows. When we were short $600 one month, he went up to the attic and sold an Islander jersey that he bought years earlier at an upscale garage sale. Depending on where we were financially, we were buyers or sellers. When we were short of money, we sold. When we had discretionary income, we bought collectibles at estate sales or consignment shops or thrift shops in upscale neighborhoods. We enjoyed the hunt, and we put our findings away in the attic.

"The collectibles need to cook," Phil explained. "We'll sell them later for a higher price. Collectibles are at their height when people are in their forties. They have discretionary money, and they are nostalgic for the stuff they had in their preteens."

That explains why I searched eBay until I found a *Vogue* Ginny doll that I remembered loving. That explains why Phil saved my daughter's Cabbage Patch dolls and why they are currently back in style. That explains why Phil held onto the blue Smurfs and the pink Strawberry Shortcake plastic pieces that I called junk.

The Antiques Roadshow was popular, and we watched as people had their "junk" appraised. eBay was the only website that showcased collectibles at the time. Phil taught me how to scan and load and list. We watched incredulously as items we had put on bid up. I put a few small empty Tiffany blue boxes, which once held small pieces Phil bought me, on the auction site. I asked a starting price of ninety-nine cents. I watched the bid close at eighty-six dollars, not including shipping charges. A friend of mine bought me a Tiffany vase. I put the box it came in on eBay and watched it bid up and close at eighteen dollars ninety-nine cents. Four nude charcoal sketches I drew when I was a student at Pratt sold within a half hour to four different bidders. We were giddy. Our collectibles provided us with a slush fund that afforded us vacations.

We assumed—and you know how that goes—that we would keep supplementing our income in retirement by buying and selling collectibles, but timing is everything. As luck would have it, owning collectibles is currently out of fashion.

I started thinking about the stuff in the attic after we came home from a trip to the South. We were on the breakfast omelet line at a chain hotel. The woman in front of me turned around and asked what I was doing in Alabama.

"We're here visiting my husband's children," I explained. I had to be polite, so I asked, "What are you doing here?"

She told me she had grown up nearby but had since moved to Texas. Her mother had died, and she was there on a long weekend to go through her mother's things. "I wish I knew what the stuff meant to her," she mused. "I don't know why she kept all those things. Maybe if she had written down the stories that went with them." She shook her head. "But I don't know why they had meaning to her. I don't know what to do with all the things she accumulated, and I have to be back at work on Tuesday."

I know that I have accumulated all kinds of things and have gotten rid of all kinds of things, only to accumulate again and again and again. I bought books, and I sold books. I gave books away. I donated books. When the library was getting rid of books, I bought their discards. I bought clothes and sold clothes. I donated clothes. I bought more clothes. My walls are full of paintings and drawings I made over the years. My shelves hold things I need, but I also collected vintage tablecloths, and now I cannot remember why. I have necklaces with so-called semiprecious stones. I know where and when and why they were purchased. I have Vera Bradley bags that are supposed to be collectibles. I have some pieces of Depression and carnival glass that I inherited from my dearest aunt. I have all sorts of vases. I have a wooden sign that sits atop my office and reads "ACHIEVE."

For the love of God, achieve what?

I have my old stamp collection from when I was seven. Phil has common baseball cards from the fifties. We have scrapbooks and CDs. Who uses CDs anymore? We have seashells that I collected from every beach vacation that we took. We have seven years of tax returns. We have gardening tools that must be antiques by now. I have afghans and shawls that I knitted. They match my decor but will not match the adult children's decor. I have all the circular and straight knitting needles that I thought I would use forever. In the backyard sheds we have balls: baseballs, tennis balls, footballs, basketballs, bowling balls, beach balls, soccer balls, golf balls. I have throw pillows from every decorating and redecorating phase. I have carpets from every decorating and redecorating phase. We have playbills from all the Broadway and off Broadway shows we have ever seen. They don't take up much space and they tell a story of fun. We have lived in this one-thousand-square-foot beach cottage for decades. And yet, it accommodates all this stuff!

My mother gave me her "good" jewelry after she was diagnosed with cancer in her sixties. She replaced her good jewelry with marcasite pins, necklaces, earrings, and bracelets when she realized that she was still alive. I would love to give some of my good pieces to my daughter now, but her life is so hectic that she asked me to hold on to them for safekeeping.

Our furnishings are eclectic. Some are real antiques. Others are Ethan Allen traditional designs. Some are vintage. Some are flea-market bargains. I have oriental carpets that I won on eBay. Every item in my cottage has a story to tell. But who has time to listen now that I have time to tell the story?

I used to imagine that what we tried but failed to accomplish in our lives, would be achieved in our deaths. I imagined our adult children—my one and my husband's three—coming back to our house after the funerals. Surely they would stay and go through our stuff and talk and connect and find out who we really were by going through our stuff. I fantasized they would go up to the crawl space and pull down our photographs and lovingly turn the pages and ask questions and bond. In reality, the crawl space is full of crap that we do not use, and now, it is even more crammed with things my daughter and her family do not use. Nothing is labeled. No one could find anything up there in its present condition.

I imagined "the girls" fingering my jewelry and dividing it up. I imagined them choosing which paintings and photographs they would take back with them and keep. I imagined "the boys" going through my husband's sports collectibles and equipment and dividing them up. I imagined them sharing and swapping stories.

I sense that my imagination has not focused on the details. Two out of our combined four adult children are now divorced. Where would the adult kids sleep? Where would they sit? Where would they eat? All the adult children hold jobs. My stepchildren are not Jewish, and they will not stay for *shivah,* the Jewish period of seven days of formal mourning for the dead. They will not rummage and talk and share and ask. They live far away. They have children and demanding schedules. Their own children are not emotionally connected to us, and they will not miss us since they barely know us. We may even have to pay for them to fly in for a graveside funeral and then drive them back to the airport so that they can get back home that same evening.

My daughter will still be "the only child." The extended family that we tried to create, to blend, never completely meshed. So as I look around my cottage dwelling, it occurs to me that we have a lot of stuff. The question is, do we do my daughter a favor and get rid of the excesses and *not* replace the stuff that we sell or give away or throw away, or do we burden her by making her go through decades of our lives? To declutter or not to declutter: that is the question!

We decide to declutter. But no one wants our stuff. So now we are asking ourselves if we should throw away or not, because it costs money to throw away stuff. A dumpster can cost thousands of dollars. A friend of mine called a We-Haul-Junk company, and it cost her hundreds of dollars to have them cart away furnishings that had cost her thousands to buy. It is dawning on me that the movie *Idiocracy* may actually be prophetic. The baby boomers will be leaving mountains of garbage behind them because we were all "Material Girls," and our children simply do not want our shit.

Phil wants to know if our grandchildren will be interested in our stuff. Phil recently spent an hour with our Graham. They watched a YouTube video about old pennies. Phil let Graham discover how valuable some of them are. Then Phil showed Graham his old pennies. Graham tested them with a magnet and found the 1943 steel pennies. He got excited when he found out that some of the pennies were worth two, even five dollars a piece. We are wondering if this piece of culture, this coin-collecting hobby, is worth passing down. If Graham is interested, should Phil spend time teaching him how to research, sell, and upgrade?

Graham understood the importance of money at a very early age. When he was three, he ran into our house breathless. "Grandma," he said in a very serious voice, "I need money."

I got flustered. "Graham, what do you need the money for?" I was ready to run to the bank and empty all our accounts.

"Charlie Biggs broke my ball," he said, tears welling up in his eyes.

"What ball?" I asked, trying to figure out how a rubber ball could be broken by another three-year-old.

"I put money in the machine, and I got a blue ball." He was sniffling.

"Oh," I said, realizing. "It was a plastic ball from the coin machine."

Grandpa opened his wallet and handed Graham five dollars, and I could not help saying, "You better tell that Charlie Biggs not to be breaking your balls!"

To which Graham patiently corrected me:

"Grandma, he broke my ball, not my balls."

PEACH HEAVEN

No college professor ever taught me that there are business cycles that would affect me directly. My father was a teacher. His father was a teacher. His grandfather was a teacher. His great grandfather was a teacher in the *shtetl*, or small village, in Eastern Europe. For all I know, my great-great-great-grandfather was a teacher as well. My mother's family made their living in the arts. One cousin was an engraver. Another cousin whittled wood. Another cousin was a graphic designer. The next generation of women became art teachers.

The boys in my class were destined to become nuclear physicists, actuaries, doctors, lawyers, and engineers. I graduated from high school in 1969. The girls in my class were going to be teachers or social workers or nurses. My father was teaching middle-school English in East New York. Listening to what was going on in his classroom, I was sure I did not want to teach, but I got my teaching certificate, nonetheless, because I could not imagine myself as a social worker or a nurse.

It was not until way later, after I was well into my second career and after I had my daughter, that I realized teaching was in my blood and that I actually loved it. There were no teaching jobs available when I graduated from college. People were driving taxis while waiting for teaching jobs to open up. I knew I could not drive a cab for a living. I started painting and realized how much I loved art. I decided to go to art school for my master's degree. I took classes at the museum. I took classes at the School of Visual Arts. I drew at the Art Students League. I put a portfolio together, and I was accepted to Pratt Institute. My plan was to get a master's in art. However, a bachelor's in English literature combined with a master's in art would have made me undesirably unemployable. I switched to a major in design—specifically space planning. It was the late 1970s, and office buildings were going up faster than you could build one out of Legos. Everyone in my class was a former English teacher. Mostly we were women who were extremely excited that we would be going out into the world of business and power.

I discovered I was pregnant just as I was finishing up my course work. My first husband was a computer programmer/analyst, and he was in the right place at the right time of the business cycle. There was a shortage of techies then. The banks were only beginning to think about how to program an ATM. I was able to be a stay-at-home mom for the first two years. One day I woke up and wanted to work part-time or as a freelancer. I contacted Pratt. I contacted a few local architects and designers. One architect liked my spunk and called me in for an interview. He did not have a paid entry-level job per se. What he offered me was a "spec" job. He sent me to a client he could not close. If I closed the deal, the creative design would be my job and my calling card.

The business was a funeral parlor on Northern Boulevard in Queens, just a short drive from where we were living at the time. I was raised Orthodox, and when I rebelled, I went to Israel to fulfill my destiny as a Zionist. I had never before set foot inside a Catholic funeral parlor.

It was very quiet when I did my first walk-through just to get the feel of the place. I slowed my pace down and walked through again. I became aware that I was not alone.

Those open caskets contained people—dead people. An idea began to percolate. There was drama in Catholic funeral parlors, drama that did not exist in their Jewish counterparts. Art is drama, and drama is art. I saw two viewing rooms.

Why not focus on the subject, a voice inside me said. The subject *is* the casket with the dead body in it, open to the public. Display it, the voice said. Build a stage on the angle and put the body on the stage. Have two kinds of lighting: ambient lighting, soft, hazy in the background, and floodlights focused on the body in the casket, highlighting the reason for the gathering. Pipe Vivaldi or Mozart into the rooms. Give the body a proper send-off, the voice continued. Allude to the heaven that you yourself want to believe in. Paint the walls of one room apricot. Paint the walls of the other room raspberry. Install blueberry carpet in the apricot-colored room. Install peach carpet in the raspberry-colored room. Keep the colors soft, muted. Create the feeling of heaven here in this transitionary space.

I put a design board together. I picked out commercial stackable chairs. I proposed that they be upholstered in washable fabric in soft sorbet colors: cherry, mango, lemon, and grape. The idea was that these chairs could be moved from viewing room to viewing room, could be used to create spontaneous conversational groups within the larger space. They would be flexible and versatile and they would be soft. The whole setting would console and comfort and reassure the ones left here on earth that heaven did, indeed, exist.

The architect bit his lip. He loved the idea of the different muted-colored upholstered chairs. He was afraid it would be a hard sell.

"Get out of here," the client yelled when we went to present the idea. "Are you insane?" the client continued shouting. "My clients are used to this." And he pointed to the drab blue-and-green long drapes that hung up against the dark-brown Formica paneling. The decor looked similar to the pizza parlor next door. "Do you want me to lose my business?" he said accusingly. "My wife designed this. This is what my clients expect. This is what they want," he said, pointing again.

"Then why did you call an architect who specializes in modern design?" I asked silently.

My design teacher's voice in my head answered. When the clients ask for something and you give it to them, nine out of ten times, they will go with a designer who gives them the exact opposite of what they asked for. I was too naïve to understand that at the time. Life experience would teach me that this seemingly contradictory behavior is not limited to the design field. I have found that people often say one thing and then do exactly what they said they would not do.

My mother chose never to purchase a house. "Too much work," she said and waved her hands. "He"—and she pointed her chin at my father—"can't fix anything. All the work would fall on my shoulders," she said.

I think my mother was never clinically diagnosed as depressed because therapy had not made the advances it has since achieved. She complained every time she had to lift her finger to do something. She obsessed loudly to her sisters about the problem at hand, but she never did anything to solve it. She seemed to love wallowing in and whining about a problem. Somehow, the grumbling, in and of itself, satisfied her existence. She missed the whole point of living. She wanted, even demanded, to be worshipped simply because she had given birth. She knew how to survive, but she did not know how to thrive.

My mother's and father's families belonged to the same burial society. This society holds plots for the final resting place of all its members. Evidently, the woman who refused to buy real estate while alive paid small monthly fees her entire life to ensure that she would own real estate in the same neighborhood as her relatives in her death. This piece of real estate is out in Woodbridge, New Jersey. I can only think that the land was cheap, making the final resting place a bargain for a New Yorker. My mother and her sisters and her parents and my father and his brothers and their parents are all walking distance from each other in eternity. There are prepurchased plots ready for my aunts who outlived my uncles. My mother was totally involved with her family of origin and, by default, her siblings-in-law. My mother never included me in her burial society. I, her offspring, somehow got sprung, but her connection to me was not deep enough to merit its endurance into afterlife. Perhaps that is why I am obsessed with my adult child.

When I shared my vision of "peach heaven," one friend had an idea. He wanted to set up a fund for an annual outing for those who were going to care enough to remember him. He wanted to fund a bus and tickets to a Mets game. The invite would read, "It's on me, from the grave." It seemed—and still seems—like an intriguing idea. Phil piped in he would like to fund an annual trip to a Broadway show for the ones who would still remember him. I spoke up. I would consider sponsoring a trip to one of the museums in New York City. Each year it could be to a different museum based on what was on exhibit. My girlfriend piped up. She wanted to arrange an annual day to the beach, her favorite place for relaxing. I was sure that my generation was going to come up with unique funeral plans. I keep thinking there is a business opportunity here.

My daughter said she has no desire to go to a museum. She loves hiking. Would I consider getting buried in a park in upstate New York in an unmarked grave? Every year, she would go there and take a hike.

"Take a hike," I repeat, and I am not sure whether I am asking it or saying it.

I keep hoping to travel backward to a simpler time so that I can get buried in my own backyard.

It seems like we have been getting flyers, every other day for the past twenty years, from two vying cemeteries reminding us that we need to buy. Long Island is probably going to be underwater one day in the not-too-distant future. Should I factor that in? Phil's family is all spread out. If all we can hope for from them is a fly-by funeral, then chances are very slim that they will come to visit the gravesite. Phil always wanted to own a second piece of real estate. Every time I try to ask him, he waves his hand.

"I'll pass on it, for now," he says.

BOYS AND GIRLS

When my grandson was two years old, we purchased a series of books we knew he would love. *I'M FAST! I'M BAD! I STINK! I'M BIG! I'M DIRTY! I'M MIGHTY! I'M BRAVE!* I know they sound like porn flicks. Kate McMullan was actually writing about a train, a *T. rex*, a garbage truck, another dinosaur, a backhoe loader, a tugboat, and a fire truck. We, jokingly, said we would file the whole series under *P* for the penis collection.

My daughter prayed that the next one would be a girl because she sees how close we are, and she is hoping to have the kind of mother-daughter relationship that has evolved between us. Her prayers were answered. June, who was born in May, is her snugly baby. She plays with her momma's long hair as she nurses.

Graham has to be reminded to pick up his clothes. He needs a sticker chart and a rewards incentive to be reminded to put his toys away. You have to speak very loudly to get his attention when you ask him to do anything that he has no desire to do.

When June was just fifteen months old, she got the dust buster and sat down on the floor.

"What are you doing?" my daughter asked her as she video-taped her.

"I cleaning," she answered. "I helping Momma."

June's eyes light up when you ask her to throw garbage in the bin. You can see that she likes to feel useful. She runs to flush the toilet even as you are still sitting on it.

She loves to put her doll in a stroller and take care of it, and that baby doll is a girl. June loves to feed it a bottle. If you hurt yourself, June is the first one who comes running to hug you.

And she flirts. She flirts with her grandfather.

"Oh, Grandpa, Grandpa," she says when she sees him. She comes running to hug him. I am standing right next to him.

"Hi, Grandma," she finally says.

We laugh. Phil says she is programmed that way, that she is practicing her skills to attract a male. "It goes back to the Stone Age," Phil explains. "It is all about the future survival of the species," he adds with conviction.

My daughter is very sensitive to the remotest suggestion of stereotyping. I grew up with very limited career choices. I have no desire to peg women by gender. I wanted, needed to prove my worth. I wanted a rich, satisfying life. However, seeing the way my grandchildren interact and the way they respond to their environment, I wonder if there is a root reason for the stereotyping. I wonder if there is something nurturing that is inherent in a girl that is very different from the passive behavior of a boy who will respond when he has to. And I wonder if we should honor these differences rather than try to obliterate them.

June's second birthday was fast approaching. My daughter asked Graham what he thought June might like as a birthday present.

"I know," he said. "I think she would really love a plastic penis," he said, sure that he had found the one thing she was clearly lacking and desired.

So even though we do not stereotype, in the end, my daughter convinced Graham that June would love another baby doll, and that baby doll is another girl baby doll. We bought our little June a Lego set for her birthday but not just any Lego set. We bought her a Lego Duplo Castle Set so that she can practice her building skills by creating a palace for the princess.

Sometimes, I think, the more things change, the more they stay the same. It was just a few years ago when my girlfriend called me, exasperated. "I swear, they do not listen to me. If my brother, Norm, was talking, I swear they would nod and agree. They would listen intently. They would take him seriously."

She was complaining about her parents. They were conservative, traditional Italians who believed that girls were girls and boys were boys.

"Listen," I said. "I have a solution. Buy a plastic penis. When you have something important to say, whip that plastic penis out and put it on the table so that everyone can see it. I cannot guarantee that they will listen, but I can guarantee you it *will* get their attention."

NACHES

L ove is not enough. Discipline is not enough. My father would say that you needed "a little *mazal*, a little luck." I have been in dire situations, situations where I could have lost my life or gotten really, really sick. I have had a few close calls, a few near accidents on the road, a hiking mishap or two. I have struggled emotionally and financially.

Phil says I created my luck. Maybe I did, to a certain extent. I have learned from the school of hard knocks that I am resourceful and capable. I am tough like my mother. But I put kids first like my father. Phil had intuitively known that the way to my heart was through my daughter. He simply likes children, and he is at his best when he plays the "father knows best" role. My daughter loves him. Her children adore him.

There is nothing like children to either bring two adults together or tear them apart and nothing like grandchildren to bring two aging adults *back* together. Phil and I came together. There is heightened tension and focus when the grandkids are around. It makes you feel alive. There are so many more problems to solve minute by minute.

"Mine, mine, mine," the little one is screaming.

We are but a split second away from an event. Can we deflect it? Should we ignore it and let the two kids work it out? We are in the other room on standby. We are on call.

I am a lucky one. My daughter lets me be involved in her kids' lives. She allows me to have an influence. She asks me to stand in from time to time. She allows us to play the parents-once-removed role.

"All hands on deck," I call, and Phil comes shuffling.

My daughter knows her kids are keeping our vitality fresh.

We were on our way back from vacation with the adult children and the grandkids. There is nothing that beats taking a vacation with them. There are *four pairs* of adult hands on deck. There are *four pairs* of watchful eyes. There is the sun and the pool. There is the sand and the beach. Food and drinks are served. Everyone is at their best.

It was late at night when our plane was circling in the holding pattern before it could land. The children were tired and hungry, and vacation was over. The children were nudgy.

"Take him." My daughter handed me my grandson.

When we first met, Phil and I had no money. Divorce had left us poor, but Phil told me that he felt rich inside. I, who needs glasses both to see from distance and from close up, did not need any glasses to see what Phil was talking about. There is rich, and there is *rich*. It is nice when they coincide, but I know that I needed to feel rich, even if I could not *actually* be rich.

"Look." I pointed out the window. "From the heavens, New York City must look like a jewelry box. See the green lights? Don't they look like emeralds? See those red lights? They look like rubies. The white lights? They are strands of cultured pearls. Those sparky blue lights are sapphires. And those clear sparkling lights— those are diamonds," I told my grandson.

It wasn't what I said. It was the way I said it that captured his imagination. I like feeling rich, and I want my little Graham to feel rich, too.

I always tell my students that words are like money in the bank. Deposit them in your brain. We are in the enrichment business, after all. As the years pass since retirement, I am obsessed with passing culture on. There is so much culture to pass. There is American history, Jewish history, our beliefs, customs, traditions, language. There are the classics, Aesop's fables, the Greek and Latin root words. There are the prefixes and suffixes. There is art history. There is music and science and cooking. There are the arts and sports that can save teenage souls.

Our favorite holiday is Passover. The *Haggadah*, the book that tells the story of the Jewish people in Egypt, says that in every generation, every person must regard the Exodus from Egypt as if he or she is experiencing it for the first time. But how can one experience five thousand years of history when life expectancy is only eighty-seven years long? We need the abbreviated version, and we need to allow space for innovation.

My daughter does a lot of enrichment. My son-in-law does a lot of enrichment. We do our share. And we get *naches*.

Naches is a Yiddish word. Yiddish is a dying language, yet we keep some of it alive because the words are so on target and irreplaceable. It was a made-up language full of onomatopoeia. *Naches* means pride and gratification, especially derived from the achievements of one's children. *Shep naches* means to derive that pride and joy. I think it literally means to draw, or drink, to drink from the well of pride and joy that the children's accomplishments bring you.

Naches is the word I use to describe the sheer joy I get from watching my daughter parent. She pulls off the road to reprimand her son who is too raucous in the back seat.

"I cannot drive with that noise," she explains. "It is too dangerous for me to drive because that noise is too distracting. So let's sit here for a while. We can either continue on our way quietly, or we can sit here for as long as it takes," she tells my grandson.

My daughter was three when I said those exact words to her. We were driving back from a week on the shore in Connecticut. It was a long drive. She started screaming. I pulled off and explained the situation, lovingly but firmly.

At the time my grandson was being toilet-trained, my daughter hit a bit of a rough patch. The day care only accepted children who were already toilet-trained. My grandson was fine with number two but reluctant when it came to number one. When I was parenting my daughter, I always tried to make the punishment fit the crime. But these days, we have all bought into the rewards program, not unlike the credit-card companies who "reward" its users for good behavior (i.e., shopping—a lot). My daughter, like me, does not believe in rewarding good behavior just for the sake of it. Children must learn to behave properly simply because they must. However, my grandson is very strong willed, and he, willfully, did not pay attention to his toilet training.

When he was getting trained for number two, Graham spent an awful lot of time playing with Play-Doh. That made a lot of sense to me. Graham did not want to run to the toilet every time he had to pee. My daughter made a chart. He earned one sticker if he needed to be prodded or reminded and two if he initiated. As a teacher, I was so proud of her for differentiating between those two behaviors. There is nothing as wonderful as recognizing that initiating an action is more significant than following directions. He had a choice between two kinds of trucks as his reward. (Kudos to my daughter for limiting his number of choices.) She placed a picture of what he chose at the top of his chart, and he had to place and count the stickers himself. (My daughter threw math skills and elementary financial planning in to boot!)

For controlling and mastering his urinary urges, my grandson chose to reward himself with a fire truck, one that was *fully* operational with a hose that squirts real water. He may or may not have learned the early concept of symbolism, but I was so proud of my daughter. She is my daughter, only one step better.

Never mind all the catfights my daughter and I had, have, and will continue to have. When she has an agenda (and doesn't she always have an agenda) and I do not live up to her agenda, she has a temper that flares and explodes within seconds. How dare I question her! How dare I ignore her! How dare I not jump on board! How dare I simply say no! Everything is fine until I ask (not even demand) something of her that she has not expected. Then she turns on me, ready to chop my head off for a crime I did not even know I was committing. She accuses me of things that were never my intention. I am surprised you have not heard our screaming matches. I am surprised you have not heard me crying my eyes out.

Never mind that my grandson is a little passive-aggressive and does not hear what he does not feel like doing. Never mind that my granddaughter is a little out of control, and no matter how hard you watch her, she is fearless and sometimes ends up in the emergency room.

"The well is deep," I keep telling my daughter. "Our hearts are full."

Naches comes from the Hebrew root word: *Nachat. Nachat* in Hebrew means "calm rest."

"Be assured," I want to tell my daughter, "I will be able to rest calmly when it is my time because of the *naches* you give me."

Because she *is* a good mother, who is raising children who are themselves pieces of work, and still she keeps trying.

PASSING THE BATON

It is a rite of passage, like a bar mitzvah, like getting married, like having a baby shower. But there is no party. There are no presents. No one is congratulating me. It is a silent rite of passage as I pass this baton.

It is the first time my daughter steps up to the plate and invites us to her *seder*. I am delighted that I do not have to bother with all the preparations. I am glad to be able to drop some balls from my to-do lists. But as the holiday nears, I realize it is complicated. My daughter absolutely sees how dangerous religions are, how divisive the doctrines are, and she worships planet earth. We mention God a lot in the *Haggadah*. Will we even read the *Haggadah*?

My son-in-law is not Jewish, and while he has always played a great guest, how will he play host? Even if he were Jewish, he will be head of the men at the *seder*, and my daughter will be the *baalat bayit*, the *balabusta*, the mistress of her home. And in Judaism, believe me, the woman rules. I might feel diminished, insignificant, irrelevant, someone whose time has come and gone. I might feel relieved. My body might thank me for not having to stand long

96

hours on the hard tile kitchen flooring. My wrists might thank me for sparing them the cutting and chopping. Phil will be thrilled that he need not run out to buy those odds and ends that I need as I start cooking but forgot to include in the major shopping.

If I let myself, I will acknowledge how proud I am of my daughter for carrying on the traditions I hold dear and for executing them in her own style. I will be proud of my grandchildren for any reason, and participating in my favorite holidays will make me *kvell,* or burst with pride. I will be proud of my son-in-law for his generosity.

I might, however, feel like they did not do it exactly perfectly, which of course, would be my way. I must bite my tongue, I remember. I should be and am extremely grateful that I am included in my daughter's life and that she values how much I mean to her children. I know women whose daughters exclude them from sharing their husbands, their children, their holidays, their lives.

As selfish as it is, I want to honor all my ambivalent feelings, because even as I am thrilled, I am also sad. It is a loss of a role and importance. It is a silent acknowledgment that I am, indeed, aging.

But wait, my daughter is calling me. She wants me to bring the appetizers and the desserts. She wants me to prepare the special *seder* plate. She wants me to also bring the *matzo* plate, with the *matzo* cover. She wants me to bring the worn and stained *Haggadahs.* She wants us to come early because she needs our help.

THE GARDEN

The summer after my daughter left for San Francisco, when she was twenty-two years old, I was lost. I was sad. It was a beautiful day. I should have been outdoors. I should have been at the pool. I should have been sipping an iced tea under the umbrella on my deck. Instead, I lay listless on the sofa in the middle of the day, watching HGTV. The windows were shut tight. The air conditioning was on. I heard knocking. I went to see who was at the front door. No one was there. I lay down again. I heard the rapping, tapping sound again. I looked up. A huge monarch butterfly was banging against the glass in a casement window. It was July, too early for monarchs. It was banging repeatedly, even purposefully. I went out and sat down on my front stairs. The monarch butterfly landed next to me. It kept me company for a very long time. I looked at my front lawn. I was not good with grass, but I loved flowers. I was inspired. I would turn my front lawn into a perennial flower garden. The monarch flew away. As I went inside to make a plan, I noted the date on the calendar, and I stopped in my tracks. It was *exactly* a year since my friend Peggy had last visited me before she died.

Four years earlier, when Peggy was forty-three, she was diagnosed with colon cancer. I had helped her the only way I knew how. I brought her fifteen books from the library that dealt with alternative colon-cancer treatments. The office staff was horrified. It was politically incorrect to confront the situation head on. But Peggy took those books home, and her husband, a lawyer who understood research, studied them and went beyond. Peggy underwent treatment—both conventional and alternative. She traveled the world and joined a choir. She performed on stage. Peggy continued to live life to the fullest for the next four years. The summer she came to visit me, her energy was waning, and she had little patience. Peggy had always been polite and sweet, and we never mentioned death that day, but it loomed large in the space we were sharing, only I had not fully realized it at the time.

The next time I saw Peggy was at her wake. I swear she turned her head, winked at me, and rolled her eyes at the woman who was kneeling before her crying. I understood she was communicating with me. She wanted to laugh with me at this woman's hypocrisy. To tell the truth, I was a little freaked out. I told Phil what I had seen. He listened and nodded. Even though he himself did not experience it, he was open to my having experienced it. I told you, I have no choice but to love him deeply.

I chose to speak to Peggy, but silently in my head. I was uncomfortable even though I was not scared. I knew that Peggy would understand that the line between the living and the dead is not meant to be crossed.

Peggy had called me when it was clear that she was not going to make it. I shared my acupuncturist's contact information with her. Peggy saw her first once, then twice, and later, three times a week. One day, Peggy asked her husband to help her shower. She put on clean pajamas. She lit her favorite scented candle. She put on her favorite music. She said good-bye to her kids. She stayed in her husband's arms for a while, and then she said good-bye to him.

Later, my acupuncturist shared with me that Tibetan monks aspire to die calmly and peacefully in the manner Peggy had managed. My acupuncturist said that very few monks were actually able to achieve that goal. Someone once told me that people die the way they lived. Peggy had always been graceful, thoughtful, and gracious. Peggy identified with butterflies so much that later our school honored her by installing a stained-glass monarch butterfly in the window of the door to the office where she had been proud to be a school secretary.

I ripped out every blade of grass with my bare hands that summer. In the fall, I planted a perennial garden to attract butterflies. I planted ornamental grass and sedum. I planted daisies and Montauk daisies. I planted Russian sage and black-eyed Susans. I planted purple Echinacea and lavender. I put in lamb's ear, indigo, phlox, and daylilies. Peggy had been a gardener. Her backyard was host to hundreds of tulips in the early spring. I understood that it was time to let go of things in order to let them grow as they were intended to do. I opened my arms wide and let my daughter fly away. I asked Peggy to watch over my daughter from above, and I prayed that eventually she would help bring my daughter back to me.

Peggy and I had never gone out for coffee; we never chitchatted. We did not know each other's secrets. But Peggy had supported me emotionally when my daughter had been a wild teen, and I helped her when she needed it.

Every April the garden starts to take shape. Perennials only bloom for a short period. Therefore, I orchestrated the plantings so that every three weeks, new blooms come out just as the older ones fade. It is a silent concerto of color that lasts six months. Passersby stop to admire it. Phil takes pride because we have "curb appeal."

My grandson has performed dozens of science experiments in my garden. He has shut his eyes and tasted different herbs and identified them. He has discovered a world of bugs. Together, we have researched good bugs versus bad insects. We caught and identified the ten best garden bugs along with the ten worst garden bugs. Ladybugs are a gardener's best friend. We discovered that baby ladybugs, which are black with tiny yellowish spots, love to settle on daisy blossoms. Lacewings are by far the most beautiful of the good garden bugs. They have a green body with delicate white lacelike wings. Luckily, lacewings and ladybugs eat aphids and spider mites, two of the gardener's worst enemies. We caught a cricket and made a home for him. We caught fireflies and let them go. We found ants that I thought were termites only to find out that they were citronella ants. Who knew there was a species of ants that smells like lemons? We observed snails under a magnifying glass. We found a cicada shell. One August night, we stayed up extra late and admired a supermoon together.

While we are in the garden, I remind Graham that he is named after a famous author. Then I tell him that my father's name was Jerome. *J* and *G* are not that different as far as letters go. Graham has an *r* and an *m*. So does Jerome. Graham might not have been officially named after my father, but there are similarities in their names, in their personalities, in their interests, intelligence, and in the fierce love I feel for them. I want my Graham to have roots. I am a gardener, and I know that the deeper the roots, the stronger the plant.

Signs of an afterlife are everywhere. But you have to look for them. You have to be open to receiving them. You have to be prepared to recognize them when they come because they are always implied, and by the time you ask if they are real, they are gone.

When my beloved aunt Mimi passed away, we met at the *shul*, or orthodox synagogue, where she had been a member. After the service, I joined the family in the hall for a light bite. My aunt's body was being flown to Israel for burial. While I was sitting around, an orthodox man, who actually looked very much like my aunt, *if* she were disguised as a rabbi, came in and wanted to partake of the bagels and cream cheese. He wore clean clothes. He did not look shabby. My uncle, Mimi's husband, asked him if he was a member. The man said he was not. My uncle asked him if he was a family friend. The man said he was not. My aunt would have graciously invited this man to share the meal. My uncle turned him away because he thought he was a *schnorrer*, a beggar, a scrounger, who just wanted a free meal at the expense of the family. I was sure that this "orthodox man" was, indeed, my aunt, who was allowed one return visit because she had unfinished business with my uncle when she died. I felt she was given one last chance to see her husband for who he really was—a friendly man with no depth and a selfish heart—a man who elevated himself by casting aside another man whom he deemed weaker than himself. I believe my aunt was allowed to return to see him this one last time so that she could let go of her anger, her resentment, and accept him with all his glaring flaws.

Years later, this same aunt came to me in a dream and told me to read Jules Verne's *Twenty-Thousand Leagues Under the Sea*. The message for me was real. My aunt was telling me to let go of my divorce and anger, and the part of me that was seeking revenge before it consumed me. She also might have been telling me that she herself let go of her resentment and anger and that she finally accepted my uncle and his decision to remarry without seeking revenge. The lessons of the book were applicable to both of us. Upon her death, my aunt was deemed a *tzadeika*, a righteous woman, by her rabbi and community, and she was buried as one.

I have had eight such after-death experiences at various times during my life. I do look for them, but when they happen, they always catch me off guard. A few days after my father died, I felt his presence at the foot of my bed. He stayed awhile. I was upset with him for dying. But later that spring, I felt a force stronger than myself push me to get into the car and guide me to the Kindred

Spirits Annual Picnic in Central Park. I felt drawn to the stranger who was carrying the book *What They DON'T Teach You at Harvard Business School,* and while I was ranting and raving, I was acutely aware that I could not move because I felt a magnetic force surrounding us.

I thank my father for that match every day. I realize that I am more open to these weird experiences than most, or at least, I am willing to talk about them and recognize them as signs. I am awed. I believe. I share them with Phil, and he does not think I am insane. But the funny thing is that, after a little while, I myself lose faith. "What a piece of work is man" (or in this case, woman).

THE NEW NORMAL RAISES NEW QUESTIONS

I was shocked when I saw some of my pubic hairs turning white. No one had ever mentioned that would happen. So the first time I looked down, I was totally unprepared. The first thing I wondered was, are there any dyes for that area? And then I wondered what color should I dye my thinning bush.

"So what?" A girlfriend tried to comfort me. "Does Phil need reading glasses to see close up?"

"Yes," I answered.

"He is not going to put on his reading glasses to look at your pubic hair, is he?" she asked, and somehow that made sense.

Until recently, I would talk, and Phil tuned out. Now, Phil talks, and I swear I can't hear him—literally. Phil used to snore. Maybe he stopped, or maybe I am just that deaf. Who knows?

We have two bathrooms. Never mind that my bathroom is in Phil's office, and his bathroom is adjacent to our bedroom. His bathroom has the tub and a Toto toilet that is low to the ground.

We installed a grab bar next to it long before Phil was diagnosed with Parkinson's. I am told that the older we get, the easier it is to poop on a low toilet. Who knew, and who wanted to know?

And why do I hear my two-year-old granddaughter's voice say, "Mine, mine, mine," whenever I see Phil get up to use my bathroom?

Back to hair: oh sure, I have a mustache, and I pluck or thread or wax the hairs off my chin. Surely Phil trims his bushy eyebrows and his nose hairs. Surely I tweeze my two nose hairs. But why is there one hair growing on the outside of my nose near my cheek?

I could not lose the weight I wanted to when my daughter got married. I was afraid of the amount of Botox it would take to erase all the lines from my face. I did the next best thing. I bleached my teeth, and my pearly whites made me look younger. I felt good for a while. Now I expect people to get up and give me a seat on the train or bus, no matter how luminous my teeth may be. I accept and am gracious on the outside, but on the inside, I resent that it is so obvious. Will I get my eyes done one day?

When did the pill boxes, the vitamins, and all the supplement bottles take over the dining area? When did the blood-pressure monitor take up residence on the dining-room table? Whose house is this anyway?

We both soak our feet, Phil in the tub and me in the foot spa that Phil bought me a while ago. We add Epsom salt and wait for the aches and pains to go away. Then I clip Phil's toenails, and he rubs cream on my feet. Is that sexy?

The older I get, the less patience I have for what my father called *narishkeit*, or nonsense, or what I call bullshit. Every day I find I have a new pet peeve. I am angry at our government for issuing Medicare cards with our names, our Social Security numbers, and the month and year of our birth prominently displayed. It is a disaster waiting to happen, because just as I am becoming more forgetful, my identity seems to have become more exposed. Whom do I call to complain about that? And what was our government thinking?

I need a password for every device. I need a password for my servers. I need a password for my e-mail accounts. I need a password for my medical records, my insurance accounts, my Amazon Prime account, my bank accounts, my brokerage accounts. Each password needs to be at least six characters long. The passwords must contain letters and numbers. Some sites recommend they contain characters. Each password must be distinct. You are not supposed to use personal information. I need to remember each password and which account it goes with. I need to store them in a secure location, and I need to be able to access them easily. Really?

Phil's Parkinson's is affecting his lower body rather than his upper body. I have a torn meniscus. We both find the angle of getting in and out of a car very difficult to maneuver. Cannot car designers take that into consideration?

I almost choked on a piece of chicken. I thought I was going to die. I whispered, "Do the Heimlich on me." Phil started *patting* my back. I bent over the sink and coughed enough up to survive. The rest went down and scratched my throat. The next day we both watched a how-to on YouTube and refreshed our memories on how to administer the Heimlich maneuver. Do I qualify for Life Alert now?

When should I encourage my daughter to invest in the companies that make adult diapers?

When should I give in and stop worrying about my weight and make those brownies that make one feel happy?

Will I become a cantankerous old lady? Will sweet-natured Phil become a curmudgeon? Will I end up living in a house with overgrown bushes and weeds? Will I be "the cat lady?" Will I end up with *farbissina punim,* a forbidding, embittered face?

THE FINAL CHAPTER

"When you are really old," my grandson says to me, "you will die."

I swallow. I know I am staring down the barrel of a gun, so to speak. But does he *really* know this? I don't know what I should say. So I reiterate that every living thing dies but that I am not very old. Then I say, "Do you know how much Grandma loves you?"

He laughs, throws his head back. "The whole world." He laughs as he throws both arms back to demonstrate.

I plant a *geschmukteh* kiss on his forehead. *Geschmukteh* in Yiddish means tasty, delicious. My paternal grandmother was as warm as my maternal grandmother was cold. When she visited, she would plant an intense kiss on my forehead or cheek, and she would say, "Ah, *geschmukteh*," thus letting me know that she thought I was delicious.

The kiss and the word are forever entangled in my mind, and since no one in the next generation knows Yiddish, I reinvented the word so that it will forever be remembered, albeit never used properly. Nonetheless, my grandchildren will know a *geschmukteh* kiss when they get one.

If people do indeed die the way they live, then how will I die? Phil has lived his entire life in a *fertummelt,* or oblivious state. He will be lucky to die in a *fertummelt* state. I have always been a planner. How can I even fathom planning my demise?

Of course, we have a plan. We have small life-insurance policies on ourselves for each other. If one of us goes, the other one will buy a one-bedroom co-op and rent our house out. Our paperwork is all in order, but we still do not have the plots. Now that it is clear that Long Island will be under water at some point in the not-too-distant future, the park in the Catskills is looking more interesting, and then my daughter will be able to take that hike. We will have graveside funerals. Who needs a hall? But what if it snows or rains or the ground is frozen? We bury our dead quickly.

I would like to die in Phil's arms. He is the glue that holds me together. If I die first, my daughter has claimed him as her responsibility.

"I got it, Mom," she says, raising her hand, volunteering as if she is still in school. "Phil is mine."

If Phil dies first, I am screwed. No one has yet claimed me. People are aspiring to live to a hundred. I don't want to linger. It is always good to get out at the top of your game because then people remember you fondly. On the other hand, I want to attend my grandchildren's college graduations and weddings. *Death Be Not Proud* should be mandatory reading and is appropriate for everyone, no matter how old they are when they die.

Defending Your Life comes close to what I believe in. After all, I believe in education. I believe that we are here to learn. So if there is an afterlife, it would look a lot like continuing education.

"Phil," I say, "I have lived so many lives in this one life. This life is so imperfect, so hard; if the angels want to send me back, I will simply refuse."

Phil is content with a lot less than I am. He can't fathom passing on another shot at life.

"Okay," I say sometimes. "I will come back for you. But you have to wait for me. Don't go off and get married before you have grown up."

"How will I recognize you?" Phil asks.

"You just will," I say. "And we will have children together, and they will go to the best colleges and universities. So you will have to have a really good, steady job the next go-round."

Well, that is, if robots have not taken over, and jobs still exist. Of course, if there are no jobs, Phil will not want to come back, and then I will be off the hook.

There are three words for soul in Hebrew, representing the three parts of the soul. *Nefesh*, which comes from the root word "to rest," is the lowest element of the soul. You can feel it when you are well-rested. *Ruach*, or spirit, is the intermediary level. The highest level is *neshama*, which comes from the word "to breathe" and implies the part that God breathed in to form the individual soul. Does the soul split into these three parts after death? I cannot get a straight answer from any source, from any rabbi.

When I put my dear little furry friend Tigger down, I felt his *nefesh* depart his body and hover. I even thought I saw it. When we buried him in the backyard, I felt Tigger's soul standing over his body, trying to figure out what had happened.

Maybe the *nefesh* part stays on earth. Maybe that is the part that gets reincarnated. Maybe after the third *gilgul*, or cycle, it becomes part of the elements. Perhaps the *ruach*, or spirit, becomes part of the universe. Maybe the *neshama*, the part that comes directly from God, goes back to God directly. The Kabbalists believe in reincarnation. It is called *gilgul neshamot*, or the transmigration of souls. Souls return to live as part of a continuing education program. The purpose of reincarnation is for the soul to make a *Tikkun*, a correction. In other words, Judaism is a religion of second and even third chances. Judaism does not dwell on sins. One is not punished or rewarded for deeds. Judaism focuses on life and on self-improvement. The soul, if sent to *Gehenim,* or hell, is sent for a limited time in order to feel its sins. Hell is not eternal but a space and a place to relive mistakes in order to learn from them, so that the soul can be cleansed, reincarnated, and do better the next go-round.

I envy the ones who have faith. They are not tortured the way I am. I believe, but without proof, I have no faith. And yet, without hesitation, with utter conviction, I tell both my grandchildren, even though the little one is way too young to understand:

"Grandma will always look out for you, even from beyond." And then I plant a *geschmukteh* kiss on their foreheads, and we laugh.

51624970R00066

Made in the USA
Middletown, DE
13 November 2017